Data Communications Concepts

by
The Technical Publications Department
of
NCR Corporation

24 - Jan -

Howard W. Sams & Co., Inc.
4300 WEST 62ND ST. INDIANAPOLIS, INDIANA 46268 USA

Copyright © 1971 by National Cash Register Co.,
Dayton, Ohio

FIRST EDITION
FIRST PRINTING — 1978

International Standard Book Number: 0-672-21547-0
Library of Congress Catalog Card Number: 78-56160

Printed in the United States of America.

Contents

SECTION A

VERBAL AND VISUAL COMMUNICATIONS.................. 7
Verbal Communications Processes — Visual Communication Processes —
Summary

SECTION B

COMPUTERS AND COMMUNICATIONS.................... 15
Simple Mechanical Computers — Electronic Computers — Computer Communications — Computer and Communications at NCR — Summary

SECTION C

TELEPHONE SYSTEMS............................... 21
Direct Telephone Systems — Switched Telephone Systems — Telephone
Companies and Regulations — Summary

SECTION D

CIRCUIT TERMINATIONS AND MODES OF OPERATION........ 27
Communications Circuits — Modes of Operation — Balanced and Unbalanced Terminations — Dedicated Lines — Summary

SECTION E

CONVENTIONAL INTELLIGENCE SIGNALS................. 34
Voice Characteristics — Bandpass and Bandwidth — Voice Transmission
— Facsimile Transmission — Teletype Transmission — Data Transmis-
sion — Transmission Rates — Summary

SECTION F

MODULATION METHODS AND TECHNIQUES............... 49
Carriers and Modulation — Amplitude Modulation — Frequency Modulation — Single Sideband — Frequency Shift Keying — EDP Technicians
and Transmission Problems — Summary

SECTION G

BASIC CARRIER SYSTEMS............................ 70
Time Division Multiplexing — Frequency Division Multiplexing —
Groups, Supergroups, and Mastergroups — Systems Using the Public
Switched Network — Summary

SECTION H

BASIC CHARACTERISTICS OF A WIRE TRANSMISSION LINE... 83
Resistance — Reactance — Impedance — Impedance Matching — Summary

SECTION I

THE DECIBEL, A RATIO OF POWERS...................... 96
Bels — Determining the Logarithm of a Number — Decibel Case Studies
— Summary

SECTION J

A SURVEY OF TRANSMISSION PROBLEMS................. 111
Attenuation — Noise — Crosstalk — Echoes and Reflections — Delay —
Other Transmission Problems — Summary

SECTION K

CORRECTIVE ELEMENTS IN TELEPHONE CIRCUITS........ 141
Amplifiers — Impedance Matching Devices — Filters — Equalizers —
Echo Suppressors — Companders — Summary

SECTION L

INTERPRETING CIRCUIT SPECIFICATIONS................ 159
Selecting a Service — Circuit Designations — General Characteristics —
Attenuation Characteristics — Delay Characteristics — Noise
Characteristics — Summary

SECTION M

MODEMS ON DATA TRANSMISSION...................... 171
Basic Modem Characteristics — Modes of Operation — Reverse Channel
— Modem Testing and Troubleshooting — Summary

FINAL EXAM 188

APPENDIX I

REFERENCE DATA 190
USASCII Code Chart and Abbreviations — Standard Interface Connections International Alphabet No. 2 Teletype Code (Baudot) — Wire Gauges Reference — Common Logarithms — Ratio to dB Quick Conversion Chart — DBM Quick Conversion Chart — Reference Data-Formulas

APPENDIX II

GLOSSARY OF EDP COMMUNICATIONS TERMS 197

APPENDIX III

ANSWERS TO QUESTIONS 205

Verbal and Visual Communications

The first communications between members of the human race were in the form of gestures, changing facial expressions, and basic sounds. As time passed, man found these forms of communication inadequate for expressing himself. Since the number of gestures and facial expressions is limited, he developed modifications to the basic sounds to relay his ideas, feelings, and thoughts. Vocabulary, however primitive, had been invented.

Man's vocabulary was expanded in the years which followed. New words were added to describe objects and events in his environment. He began to rely more on verbalization than other forms of communication. Languages which are in use today are further expansions and specializations of basic vocabularies, and these are being modified almost daily. Verbal communication is still one of the most important means used by man to impart information.

Communications among people always involve one or more of the senses. Voice communication is not possible without our sense of hearing. Another of the senses, sight, is equally important to communication of a different form. Ideas and information are conveyed by sight in visual communication.

With the invention of vocabulary, records of history began to accumulate. Information was passed on verbally from one generation to another. A significant advance occurred when man found a way to store information for long periods of time. He began to leave markers and draw pictures which represented information. With this invention, man extended his ability to communicate. He combined the verbal and visual communications processes into one. He could compile information in greater volume and with more accuracy than before. Once he initiated a communication, it was subject to interpretation by many people over a long period of time. In addition, he could communicate over greater distances because pictures and written information could be transported from one point to another. The hieroglyphics used by early man eventually became the alphabets which are in use today.

For thousands of years, men communicated with one another, limited in time and distance by their senses. The invention of the alphabet then enabled them to store verbal information in written form and to pass it over greater distances. This communication process was still very slow, and written information was passed on to only a few intellectuals. Then came the printing press and a tremendous increase in the flow of information ensued.

In all the progress throughout history, it is probable that the most significant changes have occurred over the last hundred years. Man discovered electricity and began to find practical uses for it. When Alexander Graham Bell spoke over the first telephone, he said, "Mr. Watson, come here. I want you." Electrical and electronics devices overcame the limitations of eyes and ears, time and distance. Now a man can write a telegram at the Western Union office in New York and within a few hours it is delivered in faraway India. His television antenna, like a giant hand, snatches signals from the sky, and he can see an event as it happens in some distant place.

A man on a business trip can pick up the telephone and call his wife. He may discuss a television program he is watching which originates in his hometown. It is possible that the same television signal which he sees, and the signals which will print the weather map in his evening paper, are being transferred across the same route and through the same wires which are carrying his conversation. As a matter of fact, a telephone circuit is capable of transferring several simultaneous calls, each going to its individual destination and maintaining its own identity.

Writing, the printing press, the telephone, and the vast array of present communications media all developed because of limitations on the basic forms of visual and verbal communications. Voice communications are limited because sound seems to disappear in proportion to distance. The listener must be within a certain range of the speaker if he is to hear and understand the words. Also, the listener must have a preconceived idea of what that group of sounds represents.

VERBAL COMMUNICATION PROCESSES

There are several essential steps in the voice communications process. The first of these is the formulation of the idea or thought which will become the message. It is usually the result of conscious reflection, but it may be spontaneously produced. A man must first think about being hungry before he can ask his wife to prepare food. But the person who unknowingly sits down on a pincushion may utter a whole series of sounds, coherent or otherwise, without any real planning.

The second step of the verbal communications process occurs when sounds are generated which represent the idea. In the case of the hungry man, it might be the phrase "I want food." The sounds which make up the phrase are produced by controlled exhalation through the vocal cords, causing them to vibrate. These vibrations become a group of words making the verbal equivalent of the information or message content. This presupposes the formulation and generation of the message.

The third step in the communicating process is transmission of the information from one point to another. Transmission of the information occurs in two parts. When sounds are first generated, they modulate (vary or vibrate) air pressure at one point. The second part of the transmission of sound is the transfer of the pressure variations across a distance. There is a central area between the points which is responsible for the physical transfer of the information. This entity, regardless of its physical structure, is called the transmission medium. The transmission medium for sound is usually air; the mechanical vibrations of molecules of air cause the sounds to move from one point to another.

It is important to note that a transmission medium may be present whether sound is present or not, and that the transmission medium is in no way related to the message content. The information should be in a form (in this case air pressure variations) which causes corresponding changes in the transmission medium.

Transmission of a message does not mean that a communication is complete. Consider the drowning man who calls for help. He has formulated, generated, and transmitted a message. The transmission medium is present, and his message is relayed some distance in all directions. However, he does not communicate unless someone receives the message. The fourth step in the communications process takes place when a receiver, a person or thing, accepts the information from the transmission medium and converts it to usable form. In the case of verbal communications, the receiver is the human ear. The ear receives the mechanical vibrations from the atmosphere and converts them to nerve impulses which are passed on to the brain.

The final step in the communications process is interpretation of the message. At this point the message content again becomes important. In verbal communications the message interpretation takes place when the receiving brain conjures up the intended mental image, or recognizes the intent of the message.

The message is first formulated, then generated. The transmission includes modulation of the transmission medium and physical transfer of the information from point to point. When the message has been received and interpreted, communication is complete. Figure A-1 illustrates the voice-communication process. These are the necessary steps in the verbal communications process. They apply equally well to other forms of communications.

Any message can be intercepted at the transmitter, receiver, or any point in the transmission medium, and the most basic elements of that message can be identified and defined. When considered alone, the basic elements do not necessarily have meaning, but do contribute to the meaning of the message as a unit. In a previous example, the text of

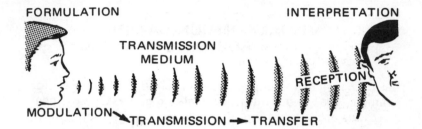

FORMULATION

INTERPRETATION

TRANSMISSION
MEDIUM

RECEPTION

MODULATION — TRANSMISSION → TRANSFER

Fig. A-1 Voice-communication process

the message was "I want food." If the words are separated, one of them considered alone does not convey the desired impression. Each is necessary within the message.

The first part of the message, the letter "I," can be further separated into two basic parts. Words are composed of pure sounds and complex sounds. "I" is a complex sound, composed of the pure sounds "ah" and "e." When pronounced together, "ah-e" becomes the spoken word "I." The pure sounds can be divided again, and the smaller parts described in terms of time (frequency), amplitude (volume), and harmonic content (multiples of a fundamental frequency).

It is obvious that messages are composed of smaller, finite elements. Some distortion of these elements always occurs. If for some reason the message content is changed or distorted in the transmitter, transmission medium, or receiver, correct interpretation of the message may be impossible. The distortion is not too important in verbal communications. For example, suppose the word "I" is removed from the message "I want food." (Loss of part of the message is one form of distortion.) The receiving person would probably reinsert "I" into the message. But that is only because his brain is capable of evaluating the circumstances which led to generation of that particular message.

VISUAL COMMUNICATION PROCESSES

Basic visual communications are similar. Suppose, for example, that two hunters are stalking game. One of them waves his arm, indicating to the other that he should move forward. When the second man realizes the intent of the motion, he can react accordingly.

The message is formulated in the mind of the first man. When he moves his arm as the signal, the message is generated. Light is reflected when it strikes an object. The reflected light is modulated in intensity and color according to the physical structure of the object, and is reflected across space. Space is the transmission medium. If the object is in motion, the modulation of the light rays change in respect to that motion, and relay the information to the receiver. When the second person's eyes receive the reflections and his mind perceives and interprets the motion, the communication is complete.

Visual communications also involve formulation, generation, modulation, transmission, reception, and interpretation of a message. But at least some of the elements are different. The transmission medium is space instead of air. The modulation method and receiving device are different also.

As before, communication can be broken down into very small elements which can be analyzed on an individual basis. The visual image is composed at any one instant of millions of reflected light rays. Each of these contains information about the object in the form of differences in intensity and wavelength. It is important to note that the communication is only meaningful when considered as a whole unit. Any one of the elements, an individual light ray for instance, contributes to the meaning of the visual image, but it does not contain sufficient information to relay the whole message.

SUMMARY

All of the examples of communication have several things in common. In each case there is a message or information which is transferred from one point to another. There is an originating source or transmitter which generates the message, and a receiver which accepts the information and converts it to meaningful form. The information usually changes form to pass through the transmission medium.

It is difficult to arrive at a brief definition of the word "communicate" which applies well in all cases. If the small elements of any message are considered as intelligence signals, communication is the transfer of intelligence signals from one point to another, including interpretation of the intelligence signals into a form which elicits either response or understanding.

Strictly speaking, the use of any of man's senses is a form of communication. Man's brain receives a constant stream of messages about his environment, and he reacts according to his interpretation of these messages. The definition of communicate is, however, an oversimplification, since it does not specify preformulation of the information. In complex human situations, preformulation of a message is prerequisite to communicating.

Since the earliest times, man has grown in his ability to communicate. He developed verbal and visual means of communications, and expanded and refined them to a point where he can communicate ideas better, faster, and more clearly than ever before. Language, vocabulary, and written forms of communications are still being improved today. So it is with the evolution of global communications systems. One system of global communications is the telephone communications network.

QUESTIONS

Answers to the following questions are listed in Appendix III.

1. Which two basic senses are most used during communications between people?

2. What factors concerning communications between people contribute to the invention and growth of modern communications systems?

3. List the sequence of events which constitute a communication.

4. M e s s a g e s a r e c o m p o s e d o f basic _____ _____ _____ which can be identified and defined.

5. Briefly define the word "communicate".

Computers and Communications

Global communication systems developing in the modern industrial world directly affect the future of everyone. Global communications frequently involve the computer and telephone systems. Use of telephone systems by computers occurred in the early 1950's, and since then the frequency and volume of telephone-system use by computers is increasing.

SIMPLE MECHANICAL COMPUTERS

Every man has a 5-digit counter (fingers) at the end of each arm. To compute the sum of three objects and five objects, early man simply counted three digits, stored them, counted five more, stored them also, and counted (one at a time) to find the sum.

The process has not changed much since then. Numbering systems were developed to increase the number of available "digits," and mechanical devices such as the abacus were invented to increase the storage capacity.

The abacus probably originated in China around 600 BC. It is a rectangular frame which has a number of parallel wires or rods mounted between two of the sides. On each rod there is a number of beads, each representing a digit, affixed so that the beads can be moved singly or in groups along the rod. Each row of beads represents a significant figure or decimal place, increasing in value from right to left.

An abacus is pictured in figure B-1. A person operating the abacus uses his fingers to move beads back and forth on the rods. Each move represents a separate step in performing a mathematical operation.

Suppose the operator wants to add the numbers 12 and 11. He first enters or "stores" one number (12) by moving to a different location (on the rods) two beads in the right column, and one bead in the row next to it. The number 12

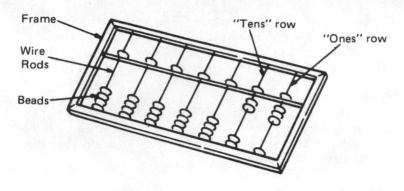

Fig. B-1   Abacus

is stored. To add 11, he moves one additional bead in each of the two columns in the same direction as before, and the number eleven is stored also. By observation — counting the total number of beads moved in each column, and assigning the appropriate decimal value — he arrives at the sum. Two beads have been stored in the second row (which indicates that the sum is twenty or greater) and three have been stored in the rightmost row (which means that the sum is three greater than twenty, or twenty-three). The process is simply to enter (or store) each sequence of digits in a number by manipulating beads in appropriate rows and to read the sum directly from the abacus. Since the number of decimal places can be increased by adding more rows of beads, computations involving larger numbers are performed faster, with less chance of error than they can be by hand or head.

ELECTRONIC COMPUTERS

With the advent and growth of electronics as an industry, man has been provided a tool which can have practically unlimited storage capacity and performs computations faster than ever. Millions of computations in a single second are possible. This tool is the electronic digital computer.

The digital computer is like an enormous abacus. The memory or data-storage area of a computer is like the frame-and-bead array of the abacus; both contain "slots" or "locations" where digits can be stored. Other areas of the computer resemble the thought mechanisms of a person performing calculations on an abacus.

The computer is called a central processing unit (CPU). Figure B-2 shows that there are three sections or functional areas in the CPU: a control section, an arithmetic-logic unit (ALU), and a memory.

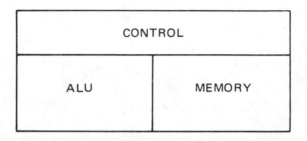

Figure   B-2   Central processing unit block diagram

Computations are performed in a manner similar to a person operating the abacus. At the command of the control section, a configuration of digits is retrieved from memory and transferred to the ALU. Another command retrieves a different configuration of digits from memory and transfers it to the ALU. A third command directs the ALU to perform an operation (add or subtract). A final command from the control section transfers the result to a location in memory where it is available for later reference. The computation is complete. The electronic finger has manipulated the beads of memory through a numerical calculation under the logical direction of the control section.

Central processing units are useless without some means of converting information into a form which can be stored and used by machines, and again converting the results to a form which can be understood by humans. Also, it is convenient to have a "file storage" area for computer

17

readable data. File storage has greater volume than the CPU memory, and is a more permanent record. Devices which perform these functions are external to the central processor and are called "terminals" or "peripherals." Figure B-3 shows how peripherals are connected to the processor.

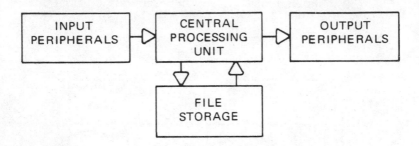

Fig. B-3   Functional elements of a computer system

Some examples of input peripheral devices are punched-card or paper-tape readers, teletype keyboards, or magnetic tape readers. Output peripheral devices include teletype units, printers, and video display systems. File storage is usually accomplished using magnetic recording devices which operate on the same principles as the home tape recorder. These generally include disc units, CRAM (Card Random Access Memory) units, or magnetic tapes.

COMPUTER COMMUNICATIONS

In early computer systems, peripherals and processors were located close to one another, usually in the same room. Information for processing was usually compiled at other locations and hand-carried to the computer room. This process was time-consuming compared to speeds at which computers operate, and it did not afford management immediate access to results.

Short electrical lines or cables were used in the computer room to connect units together. When connected in this manner and under direct control of CPU, peripherals were said to operate "online." Functions which did not involve the processor, such as printing, reading punched cards, reading paper tape, or punching holes in cards or tape were considered "offline" operations.

Since then the meaning of "online" has changed. In present use, the term means that peripherals are connected to the central processor through lengthy communications lines, each with the potential for "real-time" (instantaneous) communication through these lines (fig. B-4). When actually conversing with the processor, peripherals are "online," and when they perform operations not requiring contact with the processor, the peripherals are "offline."

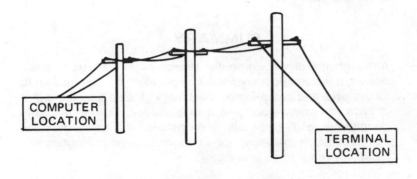

Fig. B-4 Present online concept

Of course, there are still computer or processing rooms, and a number of input, output, and file-storage terminals must be located there. But the major advantage of the present online operation is this: input and output terminals can now be placed in remote locations, miles from the computer room, and still have instant access to the central processor and storage files. A manager, sitting at his desk, can use a terminal device to search for information stored in magnetic files, or direct the processor to perform computations, and immediately have the results available. At the end of a business day, remote branches of the local bank can input to the central processing office, via telephone lines, a complete list of that day's transactions, and in a matter of minutes tallies, records and reports are checked, balanced, and available. In addition, a complete record is available from file storage for entry on monthly and other reports, and copies are printed for study and reference.

Do business machines — peripherals and processors — "converse" with each other? Do they even "communicate"? If predictable response to an intelligence or information signal completes a communication, then the machines probably do communicate with one another. Also, when computer data is being transferred through telephone lines which were originally intended for voice communications, the machines are making use of communications circuits.

SUMMARY

Although the digital computer resembles an abacus in basic design, it is tremendously more complicated. It is impractical to locate large and complicated machinery of the digital computer at each site where electronic data is needed. Therefore remote peripherals and terminals are installed at user sites for communication over telephone circuits to large computers at a location central to all users.

QUESTIONS

Answers to the following questions are listed in Appendix III.

1. List the functional sections or areas of a central processing unit (CPU).

2. List the functional elements of a computer system.

3. What is meant by an "online real-time" system?

4. Why is online operation advantageous compared to offline operation?

Telephone Systems

People throughout the world use the telephone daily without realizing the vastness and complexity of the system they are using. They are confident that when they place calls that they will be connected almost immediately, regardless of the distance or the location of the person they are trying to contact. But what are the elements which make up the telephone system? How are the connecting links formed? Who regulates telephone company operations?

From simple beginnings in the early 1900's, telephone systems have grown tremendously. In 1965 there were over 170 million telephones in operation around the world. Five countries (USA, Japan, UK, West Germany, and Canada) accounted for more than 75 percent of them.

DIRECT TELEPHONE SYSTEMS

Two telephones can be connected together using a single pair of wires for each circuit. Figure C-1 shows that connection of four telephones require six pairs of wires. Eight telephones require 28 different pairs of wires if each is able to connect to, any of the other seven subscribers (people who receive and pay for services provided by the system).

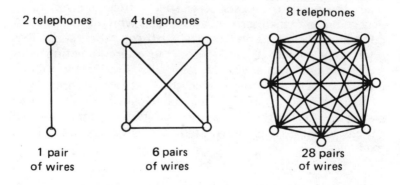

Fig. C-1   Disadvantage of direct connections

How many pairs of wires must be used to interconnect 170 million telephones? It is hard to picture 170-million pairs of wires connected to a single telephone, just to provide a person access to any other subscriber telephone in the world.

SWITCHED TELEPHONE SYSTEMS

Early in the development of telephone systems, it became apparent that an interconnection system approach was impossible. A concept was developed in which each subscriber is connected to a switchboard or "central office." When not in use, subscriber telephones are completely disconnected from the system. A subscriber, by lifting his handset, informs the central office that he desires service. The subscriber dials a sequence of numbers which direct the central office equipment to energize certain relays or switches, making connection through the maze of circuits and equipment to a single telephone. This arrangement (not to be confused with dedicated lines which are discussed later) is called the public switched network.

There is a limit to the number of subscribers which may be served by one central office, even considering "party lines" (several subscribers on the same line). A single central office may well serve a small town or rural area, but is not practical in larger cities.

Larger cities often have several central offices installed to meet the needs of subscribers. These offices are separated according to the subscribers and locales which they serve. A combination of one central office, the subscriber equipment which it serves, and the interconnecting lines makes up an "exchange." Usually, all subscribers within an exchange have the same prefix, the first two or three digits of their telephone number. Telephone calls placed from one exchange to another pass through two or more central offices. Figure C-2 illustrates the organization of an exchange.

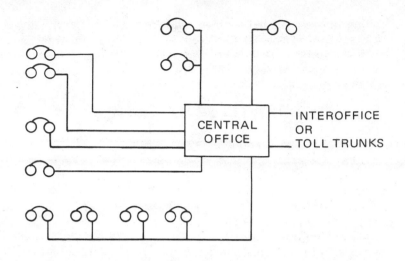

Fig. C-2   A telephone exchange

Equipment at the central office provides a number of services, including dialing, ringing, and selection of other telephones within the exchange. It also provides access to "interoffice" and "toll" trunks, which are the main routes connecting central offices and cities. Calls are relayed from one central office to another within the city through interoffice trunks, and from one city to distant places through toll trunks.

Figure C-3 shows a typical arrangement used in placing a long-distance call.

A subscriber in city "A," may call a friend in city "B." He lifts his handset and dials the number. His central office provides a connection through the interoffice trunk to the toll switchboard (SWB), which in turn provides him with one of the several trunk lines to city "B." If all of the trunk lines are busy, the toll equipment automatically attempts to establish the line through an alternate route, perhaps even through other cities. Toll equipment at city "B" then directs central office equipment to ring the desired telephone in that city. When someone answers, communications are begun. Toll equipment records the calling number, called number, and amount of time the line is used, and it provides the subscriber with this information on his monthly bill. When either party hangs up, the central office equipment disconnects the line, making it available for the next call.

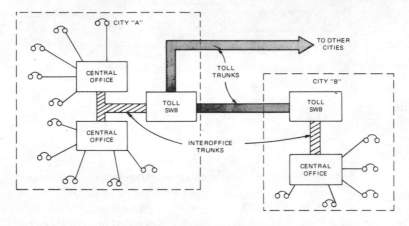

Fig. C-3   Exchange and toll system

A subscriber line probably consists of overhead or underground wires. When a call leaves the central office on the interoffice trunk, it is usually combined with many others in a multiconductor cable or microwave transmission system (microwave is a form of radio communications). Depending on the distance between the calling city and the city called, the toll network uses a number of transmission mediums, including wired circuits, microwave or radio links, undersea cable, and radio-link by satellite. The worldwide telephone system makes use of considerable equipment, involves a large number of people, and raises a number of interesting management questions.

TELEPHONE COMPANIES
AND REGULATIONS

In the United States, the telephone operations are under the jurisdiction of the Federal Communications Commission (FCC). Rules, regulations, and tariffs are applied to interstate calls according to the bylaws of the

FCC. Telephone operations within a state must also conform to the laws of that state.

The telephone companies in the United States are independently owned; therefore rates and services are not standardized. However, the rates and services from the three major companies are comparable. Those three are American Telephone and Telegraph (which includes 23 operating companies in the Bell System), Western Union, and General Telephone and Electronics.

International operations are controlled by international law. Rates, tariffs, and services are provided according to treaties or bilateral agreements between governments.

In most countries, the telephone companies are owned and operated by the government, or are government controlled. In the event of national emergency, the telephone system probably reverts to exclusive govermental use, providing a communications network for coordinating emergency activities.

SUMMARY

From a simple beginning, telephone systems have developed into very large and complex operations. There were many problems encountered early in the development which have contributed to the present structure of telephone companies and networks. Perhaps the most significant outgrowth of these problems has been the public-switched concept of operation which permits many subscribers to make use of common facilities on a time-sharing basis.

Central offices have developed as switching centers, and each serves a number of subscribers. A combination of one central office, subscriber telephones, and interconnecting wires make up an exchange. Exchanges are connected to each other in urban areas through interoffice trunks, and to more distant locations through toll networks and toll trunks. Trunks are single routes of communication which are capable of transferring many simultaneous conversations.

Rapid expansion of the telephone industry, its usefulness for military purposes, and the problems of interfacing systems within and between countries have resulted in governmental control. Rates, services, and standards of quality vary widely, but they are generally in the interest of the subscriber.

QUESTIONS

Answers to the following questions should be listed in Appendix III.

1. What is a telephone subscriber?

2. What is the advantage to the "switched" approach to telephone circuit operation?

3. What is included in a telephone exchange?

4. List four functions which central offices provide for subscribers.

5. What types of transmission mediums are possible in long-distance telephone circuits?

6. What is a communications trunk?

Circuit Terminations and Modes of Operation

There are a number of factors about connecting and operating telephone circuits which an EDP technician should know. He connects equipment to telephone circuits and he troubleshoots systems which are already operational. His proficiency increases in direct proportion to his knowledge and understanding of circuit operation.

There are several different types of circuit termination available from the telephone company. The type of termination used is determined by the communications requirements of the customer, and by the operational mode which he needs. In general, telephone circuit terminations within the public switched network are similar. But business machines often use telephone circuits which are not part of the public switched network. The type of termination and characteristics of these circuits varies widely.

COMMUNICATIONS CIRCUITS

A circuit is a closed loop through which current flows. The difference between a simple electrical circuit and a communications circuit is that the latter is a path through which an intelligence signal is transferred. A telephone communications circuit includes subscriber lines, central office equipment, toll equipment, and transmission mediums peculiar to the circuit being considered. Any equipment which is in use to connect subscribers together is part of the circuit. A communications circuit is not a simple electrical circuit since it is composed of many smaller parts which make up the communications channel.

A communications circuit may be considered a simple electrical circuit for explanation of terminations and modes of operation. A telephone circuit has subscriber equipment connected to each end. Each must make electrical connection to the circuit in some manner. If all parts of the transmission medium are combined into one group, the telephone circuit becomes a pair of wires with subscriber equipment connected to each end. The telephone company must provide each subscriber location with at least two wires. This is called a 2-wire termination.

MODES OF OPERATION

There are several communications modes which use one pair of wires. With one important exception, (reverse channel, discussed later), the information signals are transferred in only one direction at a time. If the communications objective is to transfer intelligence signals in one direction only (refer to figure D-1), the mode of operation is called "simplex." If, however, a certain intelligence signal is transferred through the circuit in one direction, and later an answer is received from the opposite direction, the mode of operation is referred to as "half duplex."

A third mode of operation, illustrated in figure D-2, is called "full duplex." This mode of operation makes use of 4-wire terminations; that is, there are four wires provided at each subscriber location. One pair of wires is used for transmitting signals, and a different pair for receiving signals. When a 4-wire circuit is operated in the full-duplex mode, intelligence signals are passed through the circuit in both directions at the same time, each through a separate 2-wire circuit or channel.

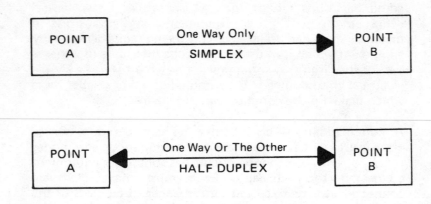

Fig. D-1   Modes of operation of 2 wire circuits

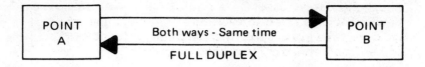

Fig. D-2   Full duplex mode of operation

Most business machines operate half-duplex through a 2-wire circuit. However, they may *operate half duplex while wired for 4-wire, full-duplex operation*. In this case data signals are still transmitted in only one direction at a time. The only difference between this mode and 2-wire half-duplex operation is that signals in either direction follow different routes (a different pair for each direction).

BALANCED AND UNBALANCED TERMINATIONS

Another important consideration regarding the termination is whether the circuits are "balanced" or "unbalanced." When the telephone company provides an unbalanced termination, one of the wires of the subscriber line is grounded at the central office, and is considered as zero volts. The signal is normally applied to the other wire as shown in figure D-3.

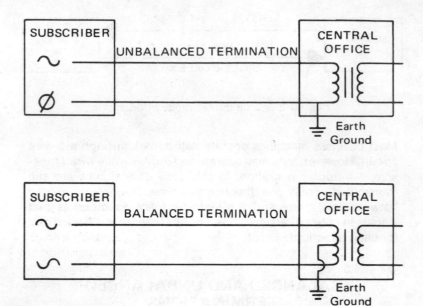

Fig. D-3   Balanced and unbalanced terminations

The balanced termination differs, as shown in figure D-3, in that neither of the subscriber wires is grounded at the central office. Instead, the circuit is connected in such a manner that the electrical *center* of the circuit is referenced to ground. Neither of the wires is considered as zero volts. Signal voltages, and currents are present on both wires when the line is in use. These voltages and currents are equal in amplitude and opposite in polarity to each other with respect to the earth ground provided at the central office.

Subscribers using the public switched circuits are normally provided with two-wire unbalanced terminations. One of the wires is grounded at the central office. A power supply at the central office normally applies 48 volts d.c. to the other wire. This d.c. voltage provides dialing and speech currents in the circuit.

DEDICATED LINES

When a potential subscriber has an application for which the public switched network is unsuitable, he may request a dedicated line from the telephone company. Dedicated lines are more expensive because they provide a full-time communications circuit for the exclusive use of the one customer. When a customer requests a dedicated line, he must specify, among other things, whether he requires a 2- or 4-wire circuit.

When the price and parameters of a line have been agreed upon, the telephone company provides the service. This dedicated channel may pass through central offices, interoffice trunks, and toll trunks, but it usually cannot be accessed through the public switched network. Figure D-4 illustrates this important difference between public switched and dedicated lines. There is no *d.c.* voltage applied to the dedicated line by either subscriber or central office. Power to transfer *a.c.* signals through the circuit is provided by the subscriber, and he is limited by agreement to the maximum power level which may be applied.

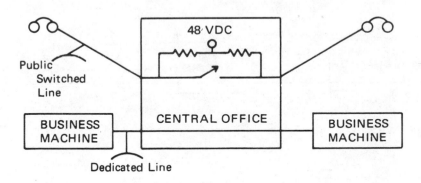

Fig. D-4   Public versus dedicated (private) lines

When a subscriber requests dedicated service, he must also state whether the circuit is to operate "point-to-point" or "multipoint." As shown in figure D-5, point-to-point means that there is a separate communications channel between any two points of a network. Communications signals are transferred between only two points at a time. A system which is connected for multipoint operation has one communications channel which connects all points of the system. The signals in the channel are received by all stations or terminals simultaneously.

Suppose a technician is required to install an online system, and that this system is designed to operate full-duplex through a 4-wire circuit. Further, suppose that it does not operate satisfactorily in any other mode. He may reach a point where he moves the equipment to separate locations prior to final connection only to find that the telephone company has provided him with a 2-wire termination. Familiarity with different operational modes and circuit configurations enables the technician to recognize such errors in system configuration, and assists him in initiating necessary corrective action.

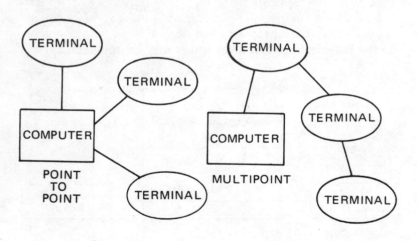

Fig. D-5   Two configurations of online systems

SUMMARY

Telephone circuits are capable of various modes of operation. If they carry information in one direction only, they operate in simplex mode. If they carry information in two directions at alternate times, they operate half duplex. If information is transferred in both directions simultaneously, they operate duplex (or "full" duplex). Telephone circuits may be balanced or unbalanced with respect to earth ground. They may be part of the public switched network, or they may be dedicated for use by individual private subscribers only.

QUESTIONS

Answers to the following questions are listed in Appendix III.

1. Describe the difference between a simple electrical circuit and a communications circuit.

2. Explain the following terms as related to communications circuits.

   a. Simplex

   b. Half-duplex

   c. Full-duplex

3. Explain the difference between balanced and unbalanced lines.

4. Describe the difference between public switched and dedicated lines.

5. Which mode of operation, point-to-point or multipoint, compares to party line operation in the public switched network?

Conventional Intelligence Signals

Telephone circuits were initially designed to carry voice signals, and the principal use of these circuits is still voice communications. But over the years numerous other types of intelligence signals have been developed for which the telephone circuits are a satisfactory transmission medium. Printed information and pictures are commonly converted to electrical signals for transmission and are reproduced at a different location. Business machines have been developed which make use of existing telephone circuits in online applications, and the number of telephone calls which transfer information in the form of EDP signals is rapidly increasing.

VOICE CHARACTERISTICS

Because telephone circuits are designed for voice communications, any other type of information to be transmitted through these same circuits must conform to the standards already established for voice transmission.

Section A described production of sound by vocal cords. But how does one sound differ from another? Why is a man's voice different from a woman's? What is it about sound which permits words to have meaning? Such questions are answered by a study of voice characteristics.

Sound is a mechanical vibration in a medium, usually air, and the waves of changing pressure travel outward from the source like waves from a pebble dropped in calm water. Waves travel away from the source at near constant speed, they have amplitude (difference between crest and valley), and they have a frequency or repetition rate (a given number of waves pass a fixed point in a certain amount of time).

The characteristics of the human voice are similar. Sound travels away from the source at approximately 746 miles-per-hour (1200 kilometers-per-hour). Loudness of a sound is proportional to amplitude of air pressure variations. The frequency of sound waves is more complex than the repetition rate of waves in water. Pure tones vary at one frequency only, but speech is composed of many fundamental frequencies and harmonics. The dominant frequency of a sound wave is called its pitch. The higher the frequency, the higher the pitch of the sound. It is the characteristic of frequency or pitch which makes one sound different from another, helps to identify people by their voices, and permits them to communicate. Two terms which are used to describe the frequency ranges and limitations of sound (or any other signal which varies in frequency) are "bandpass" and "bandwidth."

BANDPASS AND BANDWIDTH

Bandpass is expressed as two numbers which represent the upper and lower frequencies to which a circuit responds. Frequency is expressed in Hertz (Hz) or cycles-per-second (cps). A statement of bandpass which reads "from 200 to 3200 Hz" indicates that signals occurring between these two extremes pass through the circuit, but signals at frequencies outside of these extremes (for example, 100 Hz or 5000 Hz) do not.

Bandwidth is a number which describes the range of frequencies under consideration without stating what the specific upper and lower limits are. It is computed by subtracting the lowest frequency from the highest frequency within the bandpass. In the previous example the bandpass is 200 Hz to 3200 Hz. Therefore, the bandwidth is 3000 Hz (3200 Hz − 200 Hz = 3000 Hz.)

Figure E-1 illustrates the commonly used frequency range of voice and music signals. The bandpass of a telephone circuit is shown in comparison.

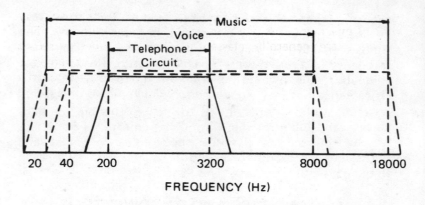

FREQUENCY (Hz)

Fig. E-1   Bandwidth and bandpass comparison

The diagram shows that ideal circuits for the transmission of music have a bandpass from 20 to 18 000 Hz, a bandwidth of 17 980 Hz. If the circuit does not have at least this amount of bandpass, some of the frequencies generated by musical instruments do not pass through the circuit. The same is true for voice transmission. If a voice circuit does not have bandpass from 40 to 8000 Hz, some voice frequencies are eliminated before reaching the far end of the circuit. The rejection of some frequencies of a complex waveform changes sound quality; it is called "attenuation frequency distortion."

A certain amount of frequency distortion can be tolerated and still leave speech and music understandable. The common table radio is a good example. It has a bandwidth of 5000 Hz, which means that higher-frequency components of voice and music signals are eliminated; yet speech is understood, and only the most fervent of music critics notice the frequency distortion in the music. Experiments with communications circuits prove that satisfactory voice communications can occur through electrical circuits if the bandpass is 200 to 3200 Hz, a bandwidth of 3000 Hz. This is a standard frequency response of most telephone circuits. These telephone circuits are referred to as "3-kHz" or "3-kc" channels.

While the 3-kHz voice channel is most common in telephone circuits (all of the public switched circuits are 3 kHz channels), it is possible to lease circuits from the telephone company which have different bandwidths. The circuits are generally classed into three groups: narrow band, voice band, and broad band. Some of the advantages and limitations of these three classes are discussed later in the chapter.

VOICE TRANSMISSION

Voice is a mechanical vibration. But circuits respond to electrical variations, rather than mechanical vibrations. Therefore, a transducer which converts mechanical energy to electrical energy must be used. The microphone is such a transducer. Mechanical vibrations at the microphone cause varying electrical currents in the circuit in proportion to the frequency and amplitude of the original sound. Electrical variations within the bandpass of the circuit are transferred to another transducer, a speaker; the speaker converts the electrical signals to sounds which can be heard and understood. Figure E-2 illustrates the basic concepts of voice transmission.

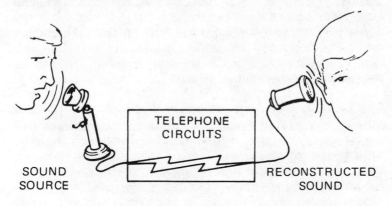

Fig. E-2   Basic principles of voice transmission

A voice signal at the transmitter appears on an oscilloscope as a waveform which constantly varies in amplitude; it is composed of many frequencies within the band of 40 to 8000 Hz. At the telephone receiver, the waveform appears different because all frequencies below 200 Hz, and those above 3200 Hz, are eliminated by the telephone circuit.

Since most of the variations generated by vocal cords for speech occur within this range, the frequency distortion caused by telephone-circuit bandwidth is not detrimental to meaningful communications.

FACSIMILE TRANSMISSION

A facsimile is a likeness or representation of material in graphic form; facsimiles include pictures or printed information. In a facsimile-transmission process, images converted into electrical signals are accepted by the telephone circuit and transmitted from point to point; then the electrial signals are used to reproduce a semblance of the original image.

The facsimile transmitter has a drum which rotates at a fixed speed, to which the copy is affixed. As the drum rotates, incremental parts of the copy are scanned by a photocell. This varies an electrical current in proportion to the amount of reflected light. Since the amount of reflected light from the image is proportional to the light, dark, and grey areas of the picture, the electrical signals from the photocell represent the contrasts of the picture. The signals are then modulated or pulsed at an 1800-Hz rate and applied to the circuit for transmission. Figure E-3 illustrates the facsimile transmission process.

The facsimile recorder (receiver) makes use of the 1800-Hz pulses to synchronize another rotating drum. The varying amplitude of the signal is then used to reproduce a facsimile of the original image on film or specially treated paper. When a photographic process is used, the facsimile signals are applied to a special light bulb which exposes the film in proportion to the amplitude of the facsimile signal. Prints are developed later in a darkroom. A different receive method makes use of a stylus to burn dark, light, and grey areas into chemically treated paper as the drum rotates.

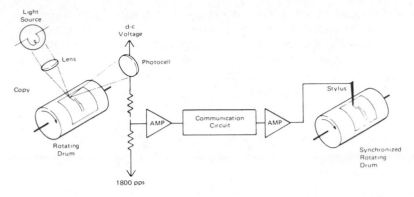

Fig. E-3   Facsimile Transmission Process

Facsimile-transmission waveforms are difficult to display on an oscilloscope. Picture information signals constantly vary in amplitude and frequency. Rapid transitions from light to dark areas, or the reverse, cause high frequency signals to be generated. More gradual changes appear as lower frequency signals. If an oscilloscope is synchronized with the 1800-Hz repetition rate, one part of the transmitted facsimile signal may appear as shown in figure E-4.

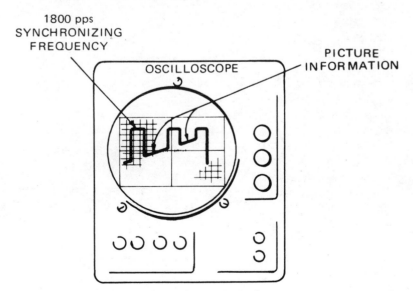

Fig. E-4   Representation of a facsimile signal

Pictures and weather maps transmitted by facsimile process are plentiful in newspapers and elsewhere and are easily identified because they appear as a maze of small dots in varying shades of grey. Telephone companies provide numerous services to news media and weather bureaus: transmission of facsimile signals for photographic and printed information, weather information, and the like.

TELETYPE TRANSMISSION

Teletype is a form of transmission in which the receiver prints characters as they are manually input to a typewriter keyboard at the transmitter location. The terminal devices of a teletype system are a transmitter-distributor, which sends information, and a teletypewriter or teleprinter, which receives and prints the information. These are illustrated in figure E-5.

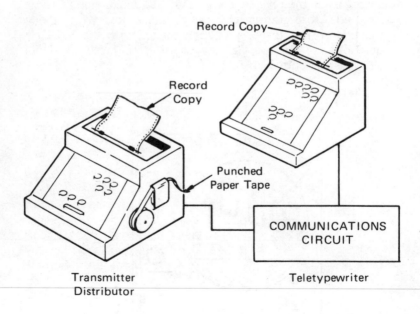

Fig. E-5   Elements of a teletype transmission system

While teletype signals *can* be transmitted as the information is being typed on the keyboard, it is more efficient to use the transmitter-distributor to punch holes in paper tape, which then contains the information in coded form. The messages are then transmitted in groups at some later time by conditioning the transmitter-distributor to automatically read the punched paper tape and generate signals for transmission. Standard transmission speeds for teletype signals are 60 words-per-minute (wpm) and 100 wpm.

Teletype signals closely resemble the data signals which are used in business machines. As a matter of fact, most of the terms which describe teletype signals are presently used to describe data signals.

There are several teletype codes in use. International alphabets number 2 and number 3 are most common. A chart showing the codes for each character in alphabet no. 2 is located in appendix I.

Figure E-6 represents the output signal from the transmitter-distributor (using international alphabet number 2) as it appears on an oscilloscope, immediately after the letter "P" is pressed on the keyboard.

The time slot of 163 msec. is called a "character," and is divided into seven increments called "bits." Initially, current flows in the output circuit while the transmitter-distributor is idle. Shortly after the key is pressed, current ceases to flow for 22 msec., generating the start bit. This causes the selection cycle in the teletype receiver to start. The next five bits of 22 msec. each represent the information, in this case the letter "P." This configuration of bits is received and stored by the teletype receiver. During the final bit time of 31 msec., the teletype receiver prints the character or number according to the bits of that character. It then coasts to a stop and waits for a new signal to start another selection cycle.

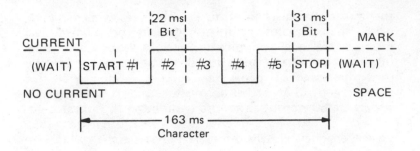

Fig. E-6   Letter "P" in international teletype alphabet number 2

Teletype characters are encoded in a format in which two conditions are possible. When current flows, the condition is referred to as a "mark" or digital "ONE." This condition is produced from paper tape if a hole is present. When no current flows, the condition is referred to as a "space" or digital "ZERO." It is produced by the transmitter-distributor if there is no hole present in the paper tape.

The "character time" of 163 msec. in the example corresponds to a teletype transmission rate of 60 wpm (a word is six characters). If the transmission rate is increased, the "character time" and the individual "bit times" must be reduced. The "character time" of a 100 wpm system is 100 msec. and the individual "bit times," except for the stop bit, are 13.5 msec.

The most technicially accurate method of determining signaling speed is by use of the "baud." Baud-rate is determined by dividing 1 second by the shortest time duration of any pulse in any one character. Telephone technicians refer to teletype circuits as "45-baud circuits" and "74-baud circuits," which refer to transmission rates of 60 wpm and 100 wpm respectively.

The term baud is also useful for calculating the minimum required bandwidth for d.c. signals. The result of multiplying the baud-rate by 3 is equal to the minimum acceptable circuit bandwidth. If the circuit bandwidth is less, the d.c. signals undergo severe frequency distortion and cause errors in printing at the receiver terminal. A 74-baud circuit, for example, requires a *minimum* circuit bandwidth of 222 Hz if d.c. signals are to pass through satisfactorily. If the bandwidth is greater, less distortion will occur.

Because of frequency distortion, d.c. signals are normally not applied directly to telephone lines. Instead, the d.c. signals are applied to intermediate devices which convert the information to audio tones for transmission. At the other end of the lines, similar devices convert the audio tones back to d.c. signals. These devices include level converters and modulator-demodulators (MODEMS).

DATA TRANSMISSION

Intelligence signals generated and used by business machines are called data. As with other intelligence signals, the transmission objective is to transfer the signals, the data, from point to point. A circuit arrangement for one branch of an online computer system might appear as shown in figure E-7.

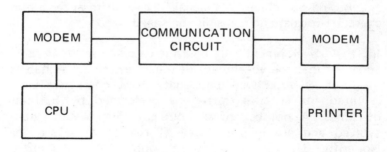

Fig. E-7   Representative point-to-point on-line system

Normally, teletype signals in the d.c. form are not acceptable for transmission through telephone circuits. The same is true of data signals. Data signals applied to one MODEM pass through the circuit and are converted to original form by another MODEM. The communications circuit shown in figure E-7 operates half duplex, point-to-point. Computer data transmitted through this circuit is in the form of digital configurations which have meaning; a "conversation" between the CPU and printer in figure E-7 may develop as follows.

Computer: "Printer, get ready to print."

Printer: "I am ready to print."

Computer: "Print a character (number 2)."

Printer: "I have printed a character."

Computer: "Printer, get ready to print."

The data signals which represent commands and answers between business machines are very similar to teletype signals. As before, two conditions are possible. The two conditions in data signals are "voltage" and "no voltage." Larger groups of bits form characters which, as with teletype signals, may represent any of a large number of letters, numbers, or symbols.

There are two major differences between teletype signals and business-machine data signals. These differences are in character format and transmission speed.

In the development of computer systems it became apparent that the vocabulary of the international alphabets used for teletype was inadequate. New characters were required for specific operations performed by business machines. A number of computer coding systems have evolved and are in use today. Three of these are the Hollerith, 315 General Purpose, and USASCII (United States of America Standard Code for Information Interchange) codes. Of these, USASCII is by far the most universally accepted; the complete USASCII code is available for reference in appendix I.

Figure E-8 illustrates the letter "P" in USASCII code. The least-significant bit is on the left as it is on an oscilloscope screen. Note that start and stop bits, bit times, and character times are not shown. These vary with individual business machines, transmission speeds, and applications.

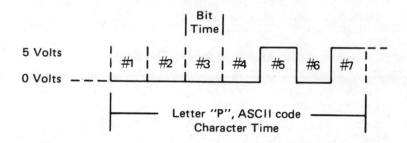

Fig. E-8   One character of ASCII code: the letter "P"

Transfer of information takes place when these 7 bits are transmitted through the circuit. A generally accepted practice is addition of an eighth bit, which is usually ignored by the receiving device. The 8-bit character is referred to as a "byte." Often, a start bit and one or two stop bits are generated and used as control signals. The specific number of supplemental bits varies with the business machine and the application.

Data-bit voltage levels are customarily assigned values of ONE and ZERO, and are referred to as "two state logic signals." If the more positive voltage is assigned a value of ONE, and the more negative voltage a value of ZERO, the format is referred to as "positive-logic levels." "Negative-logic levels" indicates that the more negative voltage has a value of ONE. Most NCR electronic business machines use positive-logic levels. Positive-logic data signals which operate MODEMS are inverted before being transmitted. The circuit normally used to accomplish this is called a level converter, and it has the additional function of changing the 0- to 5-volt levels from the business machine to the plus or minus volt levels required to operate a MODEM. Electronic Industries Association (EIA) Standard:

Digit 0 = Plus 3 to plus 25 volts
Digit 1 = Minus 3 to minus 25 volts

In a computer system, all bits have the same time duration. In Data Transmission Systems, "Bits Per Second" and "Baud Rate" frequently have the same meaning. However, some systems employ a technique called "Multi-Level Coding" and in these applications "Bits Per Second" and "Baud Rate" are not synonomous.

TRANSMISSION RATES

With the high-speed capability of modern computer systems (possibly millions of bits per second), transmission rates of 45 and 74 baud are unacceptable. Reversing the baud/bandwidth formula and dividing the voice channel bandwidth by 3 indicates that the maximum attainable transmission rate is 1000 bits per second. This is true if the d.c. levels are applied directly to the communications circuit. The use of MODEMS permits somewhat higher transmission rates. Some standard transmission rates established for data signals are 110, 600, 1000, 1200, and 2400 baud.

Peripheral devices can be separated into three groups according to transmission rates and communications requirements. Low speed devices such as the teletype can operate satisfactorily through the narrow-band circuits available from the telephone company. Narrow-band circuits are less expensive and accommodate transmission rates of up to 200 bits-per-second. Medium speed devices such as printers and video display systems generally use the more common 3-kHz "voice-band" service.

Broad-band circuits are more expensive than narrow-band or voice-band circuits, but they do provide for transmission rates of up to millions of bits per second. Whether the cost is prohibitive or justified will depend on the particular installation capabilities and customer requirements.

SUMMARY

There are several factors relating to the services and functions provided by telephone companies. The most prevalent telephone circuit, the voice channel, has some peculiar characteristics and limitations. Voice channels are originally designed to accommodate speech signals, and are adequate for that purpose. The natural development of other communications services, such as facsimile, teletype, and data-communication, leads to machines capable of communicating through the standard 3-kHz voice channel. Three classes of circuits are available (narrow band, voice band, and broad band).

QUESTIONS

Answers to the following questions are listed in Appendix III.

1. Fill in the frequencies which describe the standard voice channel:

    a. Bandpass

    b. Bandwidth

2. List four types of intelligence signals common to telephone circuits.

3. Name the terminal devices in a teletype system.

4. What is the baud rate of a 100-wpm teletype signal (start and character bits = 13.5 ms, stop bit = 19 ms)?

5. What is the minimum bandwidth required if d.c. data signals at 1000 baud are applied directly to a communications circuit?

6. In what ways are business-machine data signals different from teletype signals?

7. Which computer coding system is in most common use today?

8. What is the function of a level converter?

9. What type or category of business machine ordinarily makes use of narrowband circuits for communications?

10. What is one advantage and one disadvantage of broadband service compared to voice-band service?

Modulation Methods and Techniques

Intelligence signals in a communications circuit undergo many changes in electrical form during long distance transmission. Data and teletype signals must be changed into representative audio signals before transmission because of limited bandpass of telephone circuits. A final conversion leaves the signal, hopefully, in original form. The electrical conversions of the signal facilitate handling in the various toll systems and transmission mediums, in particular when radio systems are used.

CARRIERS AND MODULATION

Intellegence signals are transported through the telephone system in much the same way that a letter is carried through the mail. The person mailing a letter and the person receiving a letter correspond to terminal points in a communications system, and the letter is similar to the message being communicated. The mail system is the communication medium. But the mail system is not just one unit; it is composed of many smaller parts, such as the different post-office mail routes through which the letter passes.

The postmen, trucks, trains and airplanes, which actually move the letter are the carriers. The carriers are necessary in the transfer of information, but are not directly connected to the text of the letter. Content of the letter is not affected by the carriers, and it does not matter which carriers are used, so long as they move it from point to point.

Electronic carriers are similar to mail carriers. Carriers are not intelligence signals, but they are used in the transfer of intelligence waveforms. Electronic carriers convey intelligence waveforms by "modulation" and "demodulation."

Modulation is the process of impressing an intelligence waveform upon a carrier waveform for transmission. The original intelligence waveform is seldom transmitted; the information is instead contained in the modulated waveform.

Demodulation is the process of separating the information from the carrier waveform after transmission. At this point the carrier is usually discarded or eliminated because it is of no further use.

A carrier is a waveform of constant amplitude, frequency, *and* phase which can be modulated by changing amplitude, frequency, *or* phase. Carrier waveforms are usually much higher frequencies than the intelligence signal. Electronic carrier signals "carry" the intelligence signals from one point to another.

Several methods of modulating carrier signals are in use, particularly in radio systems. Each is described by a name which relates to the method of impressing the intelligence signal upon the carrier. Some of the modulation methods are amplitude modulation (AM), frequency modulation (FM), single-sideband modulation (SSB), and frequency shift keying (FSK).

When the public switched network is used for long distance calls, modulation methods may vary, and cannot be predicted. Neither can the modulation method be determined after the fact. Even if the method could be determined, technicians do not have access to the telephone circuits and equipment, and with the exception of FSK signals the modulated waveforms do not appear at the terminations.

AMPLITUDE MODULATION

Amplitude modulation is the process of combining a low frequency audio (intelligence) signal with a high frequency carrier signal to produce two new frequencies which represent the intelligence signal. The two new frequencies are called sidebands. Upper-sideband (USB) frequencies are generated by the sum of the audio and carrier frequencies, and lower-sideband (LSB) frequencies are generated by the difference between the carrier and audio frequencies.

An example illustrates the relationship between the sideband and carrier frequencies. Assume that a 2 000 Hz audio signal modulates a carrier frequency of 800 kHz. The USB frequency generated is 802 kHz (800 000 plus 2 000), and the LSB frequency is 798 kHz (800 000 minus 2 000). The bandwidth of the carrier and sideband frequencies is equal to USB (highest) minus LSB (lowest) or 4 000 Hz. Figure F-1 illustrates the relationship between the audio, carrier, and sideband frequencies.

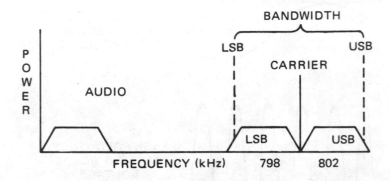

Fig. F-1   Amplitude modulation frequency relationships

The bandwidth of most commercial AM radio transmitters is limited to 10 kHz, and is centered around the carrier frequency. In the previous example the transmitter carrier frequency was 800 kHz. Therefore the bandpass of the transmitter is 795 kHz to 805 kHz. An audio frequency is *not* transmitted because it is outside the bandpass of the transmitter output circuits. The sidebands, which are generated and transmitted with the carrier frequency, represent the original audio signal.

The "modulation envelope" (shape of the composite waveform which is transmitted) varies in proportion to the amplitude and frequency of the audio modulating voltage as shown in figure F-2.

The circuit which generates AM waveforms is called a "modulator" or "mixer." The mixer has two input signals (audio and carrier frequencies) and one output signal (composite waveform). The output frequencies from the mixer include the sum, difference, and original frequencies.

The output frequencies from a mixer are the USB, LSB, audio, and carrier frequencies. Note that four frequencies are present at the mixer output, but that only three of them leave the transmitter because of the bandpass of the transmitter.

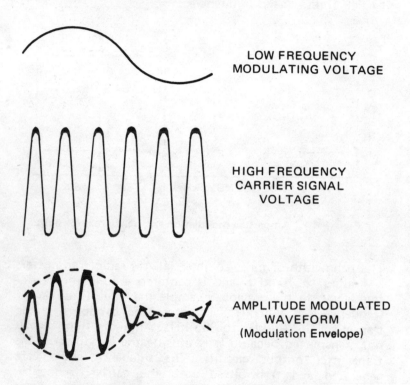

LOW FREQUENCY
MODULATING VOLTAGE

HIGH FREQUENCY
CARRIER SIGNAL
VOLTAGE

AMPLITUDE MODULATED
WAVEFORM
(Modulation Envelope)

Fig. F-2   Waveforms of amplitude-modulated signals

Mixer circuits can be constructed to operate in a linear or a nonlinear fashion. The nonlinear mixer produces the particular type of controlled distortion which we call AM, and generates sideband frequencies. The linear mixer does not produce the same type of distortion. Figure F-3 illustrates the difference in output waveforms between linear and nonlinear mixers which have identical audio and carrier signals applied. The term "mixer" in this book always refers to the nonlinear variety unless otherwise stated.

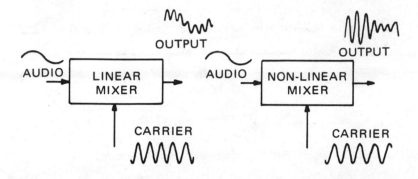

Fig. F-3   Difference between linear and nonlinear mixers

An AM radio transmitter amplifies the mixer output signal in power and applies the carrier and sideband frequencies to a transmitting antenna. The antenna is a transducer which converts the AM electrical currents to proportional electric and electromagnetic fields (radio waves) which pass through space at nearly the speed of light.

A fraction of a second after transmission, the radio waves are intercepted by a receiving antenna, another transducer. A proportional current flows in the antenna. The signal at this point is very weak because of losses in the transmission medium. It is amplified to an adequate power level by the receiver and applied to a "detector" circuit for demodulation.

The detector circuit is usually a half-wave rectifier which effectively cuts the AM waveform in half. A special filter removes the higher frequency carrier signal, leaving only a voltage which varies in proportion to the amplitude of the modulation envelope. The modulation envelope, as described above, varies in accordance with the original modulating audio signal. Figure F-4 illustrates the waveforms before, during, and after demodulation.

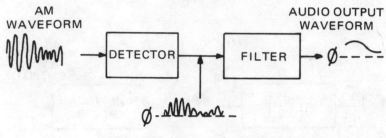

DETECTED (Rectified) WAVEFORM

Fig. F-4   AM demodulator waveforms

Commercial radio systems are one application which uses the AM transmission process. When an AM table radio is turned to 800 on the dial, it is actually being tuned to accept the 800-kHz carrier and the sideband frequencies. The audio signals (voice and music) which are heard are a result of the AM demodulation process.

FREQUENCY MODULATION

The transmission objective using frequency modulation is the same as for AM: transferring intelligence (usually audio) signals from point to point. FM, compared to AM, has certain advantages and disadvantages.

Amplitude modulation means that amplitude of the transmitted signal varies; frequency modulation means that frequency of the transmitted signal varies. An ideal FM signal is always constant in amplitude. In frequency modulation, the carrier frequency is caused to vary above and below its normal center frequency. When the carrier frequency changes it is said to "deviate" from center. The amount of deviation is proportional to amplitude of the modulating voltage, and the rate of deviation is proportional to the frequency of the modulating voltage.

When there is no modulating voltage applied, the FM

transmitter output is the "rest," "center," or "carrier" frequency. These three terms are synonymous in FM terminology. When the modulating voltage is positive it causes "positive deviation," which means that the carrier increases to some higher frequency. When the modulating voltage is negative it causes "negative deviation," which means that the carrier is decreased to some lower frequency. Power output of the transmitter remains constant regardless of whether the carrier frequency is modulated.

Figure F-5 shows how frequency modulation waveforms appear in respect to each other.

Figure F-6 pictures the results of frequency modulating a carrier signal. The composite diagram shows the FM bandwidth in one section, and the audio modulating signal below.

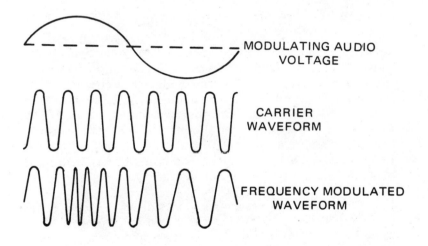

MODULATING AUDIO VOLTAGE

CARRIER WAVEFORM

FREQUENCY MODULATED WAVEFORM

Fig. F-5   Frequency-modulated waveforms

Special circuits in FM transmitters, called "reactance-tube modulators" generate FM waveforms. Other special circuits in FM receivers, called "discriminators," demodulate the FM signals.

Two main disadvantages of FM compared to AM transmission are (1) that FM signals require a much broader bandwidth, and (2) that transmission is limited to shorter range. Commercial FM receivers require a bandwidth of at least 150 kHz, and the transmission quality usually deteriorates when the transmission distance exceeds 50 or 60 miles.

But FM transmission also has two major advantages compared to AM radio transmissions. First, higher modulating audio frequencies can be used (up to 15 kHz), making the reproduction of sound more realistic. Second, because the amplitude of the waveform is ideally constant, voltage-limiter circuits are used in the receiver to clip off all amplitude variations in the signal before demodulation. These amplitude variations are the type caused by lightning and electrical disturbances in the atmosphere; as a result, FM transmissions are more noise-free than AM transmissions.

SINGLE SIDEBAND

Single-sideband transmission is similar to AM transmission, except that generation of SSB signals makes more extensive use of electrical filters. Filters are electrical circuits which are frequency sensitive, and which are used to limit the bandpass and bandwidth of other circuits as required. The four common types of filter circuits are high-pass, low-pass, bandpass, and band-reject filters. The names imply the function of each type of filter. The type of filter used most often in SSB transmission is a bandpass filter.

If a filter circuit is designed to pass only the frequencies between 200 and 3200 Hz, it is called a voice-band filter. Millions of these are in use in telephone circuits. It is possible to construct bandpass filters which will pass any desired range of frequencies, and which will block passage of all frequencies outside of this range.

Figure F-7 illustrates SSB-signal generation. A mixer is used to produce an AM waveform. The signal is then applied to a bandpass filter. The bandwidth of the filter limits passage of frequencies to the desired part of the upper-sideband (USB) signal. The USB frequencies which pass through the filter compose a single-sideband signal.

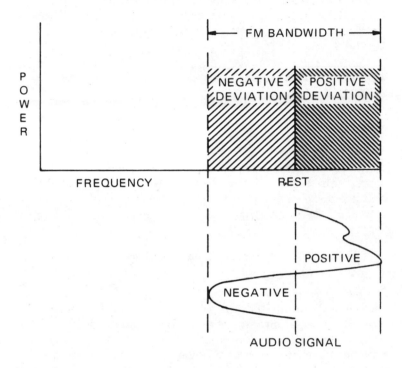

Fig. F-6   Deviation of the FM carrier frequency from center

Figure F-7 shows that only the USB frequencies remain at the filter output. One advantage of SSB compared to AM transmission is "power conservation." Since the carrier and lower sideband frequencies are not transmitted, a saving in power requirement at the transmitter results. Also, since the lower sideband is not transmitted, the SSB signal occupies only half as much bandwidth as an equivalent AM signal. This advantage is called "spectrum economy." Twice as many SSB signals can be transmitted in the same bandwidth which an AM signal requires. A third advantage of SSB compared to AM is also a direct result of using only half as much bandwidth. Noise is present at all frequencies in the spectrum. Since only half as much of the spectrum is used, only half as much noise is present in the receiver waveform. Therefore SSB transmissions have a higher "signal-to-noise" ratio than AM transmissions.

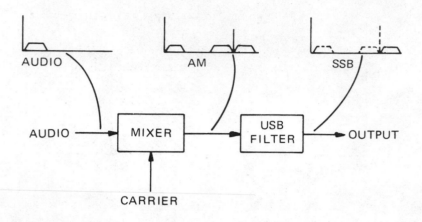

Fig. F-7 Generating a single-sideband (SSB) signal

A more common method of generating SSB signals makes use of a special circuit called a "balanced modulator." This circuit balances out (eliminates) the carrier frequency while the carrier is still at a low power level. The resulting signal, shown in figure F-8, is called double sideband (DSB). The DSB signal comprises USB and LSB signals; it is converted to SSB by a bandpass filter which removes one of the sidebands.

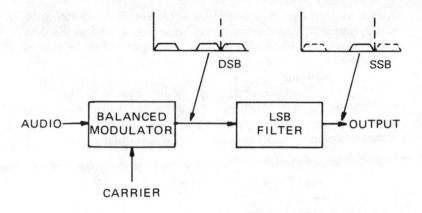

Fig. F-8   Common method of generating SSB signals

The demodulation process at the receiver is similar to the modulating process. The circuit which demodulates the signal is called a "balanced mixer." The receiver generates a new carrier frequency which is inserted into the balanced mixer stage. Mixing action takes place. One of the output frequencies produced by the balanced mixer is the difference frequency, and it is of the same frequency as the original modulating signal. Undesired mixer products are balanced or filtered out. Figure F-9 illustrates SSB demodulation.

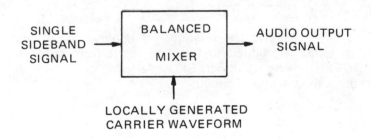

Fig.   F-9   Demodulation of single sideband signals

If the carrier frequency generated by the receiver is not exactly the same as the one which caused the modulation, audio output signals are distorted. A receiver which does not produce the carrier frequency (such as the common AM table radio) is incapable of producing intelligible sound from single sideband waveforms. These factors explain two main disadvantages of SSB compared to AM. The cost of constructing the SSB circuits is higher because of the extra circuits and closer frequency tolerances required. Also, additional circuitry is required at the receiver to ensure proper tuning of critical circuits which reduce or eliminate distortion.

FREQUENCY SHIFT KEYING

The modulation method called frequency-shift keying (FSK) is of particular interest because it is directly associated with the transmission of two-state logic signals. These are the two-condition, or binary combinations of voltages and currents which represent information in computer and teletype systems.

The FSK modulation is similar to the FM modulation technique. In the FSK modulation process, the two possible d.c. levels of the data signals are converted by a modulator to two different frequencies or tones within the bandpass of the communications circuit. A demodulator reconverts the audio tones to corresponding d.c. levels at the opposite end of the circuit. The FSK modulators and demodulators are usually contained in a single unit called a MODEM (*modulator-demodulator*).

Figure F-10 shows the relationship between a d.c. data signal which is applied to the data input terminal of the MODEM and the resulting FSK signal which is transmitted through the telephone circuit.

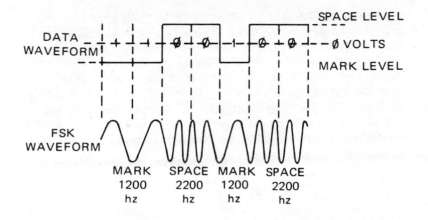

Fig. F-10   Frequency shift keyed waveforms

In the transmitted FSK waveform, the mark frequency is caused by the mark level and the space frequency is caused by the space level. If the mark frequency is transmitted for a period of time equal to two "bit times," this causes the receive MODEM to generate a d.c. logic level lasting two bit times which matches the original signal. The message content is retained through transmission of a corresponding frequency during each bit time.

Most NCR electronic equipment uses positive logic levels; the more positive level represents a binary ONE and the more negative level represents a binary ZERO. Level converters in the output circuits of the business machines invert the logic signals. After inversion, the negative level of the data signal represents a ONE and the positive level represents a ZERO. The use of negative logic levels at the data input terminals of the MODEM is, with few exceptions, a standard transmission practice. Business machines which use positive logic levels normally have level converters in the output circuits for inversion and conversion of the data signals. Inversion reverses the polarity of a voltage, and conversion changes the amplitude of a d.c. voltage. In NCR equipment, some signals are identified as "uncommon or nonstandard logic levels." This usually indicates a special inversion or conversion of voltage levels.

At the MODEM, a negative voltage is called a *mark level*; it causes the lower or mark frequency to be transmitted. Conversely, a positive voltage is called a *space level;* it causes the higher or space frequency to be transmitted. During periods of time when data is not being transmitted the MODEM usually remains locked in the marking condition. The lower (mark) frequency is constantly applied to the transmission line. Deviations from this condition represent the bits and characters of the data signals.

FSK signals resemble FM signals in that the carrier deviates in frequency. However, a true FM carrier is permitted to deviate to any other point in the channel bandwidth, but an FSK carrier is permitted to deviate to only *one* predetermined point within the channel. Since only two conditions represent the data, only one deviation from the carrier frequency is necessary.

Figure F-11 shows the location of the mark and space frequencies in respect to voice-channel bandwidth and center frequency of the channel. Note that bandwidth of the mark and space frequencies is only about one-third of the total channel bandwidth.

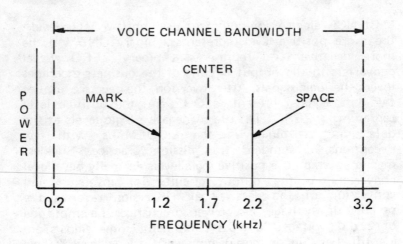

Fig. F-11   Location of FSK frequencies within the voice channel

In most applications it is a required characteristic of the FSK waveform that there is no phase discontinuity. This means that the transition from one frequency to the other must be immediate, regardless of the point in time when the MODEM is directed to cause the change. This further illustrates that the FSK output signals are at one frequency or the other, never both, and never at any frequency other than the mark or space frequency.

There are several methods of generating FSK waveforms. Perhaps the simplest method makes use of two separate oscillators, one which generates the mark frequency and another which generates the space frequency. These are connected to the output circuit by means of a switch as shown in figure F-12.

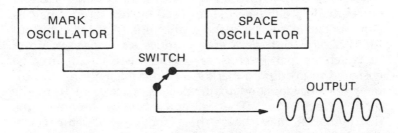

Fig. F-12   Simple method of generating FSK

Changing the position of the switch alternately applies mark and space frequencies to the transmission line. Proper timing of the changes can produce meaningful FSK signals. Practical circuits have been constructed based on this principle. The manual switch is replaced by an electronic switch, which is in turn controlled by the d.c. data levels.

The circuit shown in figure F-12 has phase discontinuity which can cause problems at the receiver. A better method of generating FSK signals makes use of one oscillator circuit. Data signals from the business machine electronically change the output frequency of the oscillator.

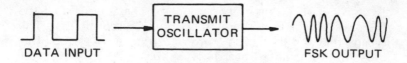

DATA INPUT   TRANSMIT OSCILLATOR   FSK OUTPUT

Fig. F-13   A more conventional method of producing FSK

Similarly many manufacturers use a type of FM discriminator in the demodulator section of the MODEM. A discriminator is a frequency-sensitive circuit. It normally does not respond to amplitude variations. The output voltage from a discriminator is a d.c. voltage which varies in proportion to the frequency of the input signal. If the input signal is a frequency-shift keyed waveform (two possible tones), the output waveform from the discriminator is two corresponding d.c. levels. The discriminator circuit may be constructed in such a manner that one of the d.c. output levels is zero volts, or it may produce an output waveform in which neither level is zero volts. The circuit may be designed to produce a mark level from the mark frequency, or it may be designed to produce a space level from the mark frequency. The circuits which follow the discriminator may have the functions of amplifying, waveform shaping, inverting, or d.c. restoration of the data signals.

Another method of demodulating FSK signals makes use of a special filter and rectifier circuit. The principle is illustrated in block diagram form in figure F-14.

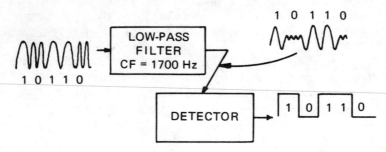

Fig. F-14   Filter method of FSK demodulation

In figure F-14 the low-pass filter has a center frequency of 1700 Hz. It passes the lower 1200-Hz mark frequency without affecting the amplitude of the waveform. When the 2200-Hz space frequency is applied to the filter, it is blocked because of the frequency characteristic of the filter, and is considerably reduced in amplitude. Since the d.c. output voltage from the detector circuit is proportional to the amplitude of the applied a.c. input voltages, the output from the detector is zero volts during the time that the space frequency is applied, and it is a positive voltage during the time that the mark frequency is applied. This action effectively demodulates the FSK waveform and converts it to original input levels.

In 1959 the United Nations extended recognition to the International Telecommunications Union (ITU). One specialized agency of the ITU, the International Telegraph and Telephone Consultative Committee (CCITT) was organized to establish standards for MODEMS and data transmission. Numerous experiments conducted by the CCITT indicate that best transmission characteristics occur when the FSK bandwidth is located around the center of the voice channel. When mark and space frequencies are equidistant from a point near the center of the band, fewer errors occur. Table F-1 shows transmission speeds and frequencies recommended by the CCITT in their publication "Supplements — Concerning Data Transmission," Blue Book, Volume VIII, published in 1964.

SIGNALLING RATE	f MARK	f CENTER	f SPACE
Up to 600 Baud	1300 Hz	1500 Hz	1700 Hz
Up to 1200 Baud	1300 Hz	1700 Hz	2100 Hz

Table   F-1   CCITT speeds and frequencies

Table F-2 shows the relationship between some representative forms of two-state signals in various business machines and transmission mediums. These agree with CCITT recommendations, but not all manufacturers subscribe to the same practices.

CODE	DIGIT 0	DIGIT 1
AM	Signal OFF	Signal ON
FM or FSK	High Frequency	Low Frequency
D.C.	Positive	Negative
Telegraphy	Space or Start	Mark or Stop
Paper Tape	No Hole	Hole

Table F-2   Two-state representations

EDP TECHNICIANS AND TRANSMISSION PROBLEMS

Technicians do not usually have access to most of the modulated waveforms. They cannot predict which modulation methods or routes will be used in the transfer of the intelligence signals. They must be satisfied with the intelligence signals which appear at the terminations as a point of reference. Knowledge of transmission techniques, however, is helpful to the technicians indirectly. When the input and output signals at the terminations differ radically from each other, becuse of distortion introduced by the transmission medium, technicians must be able to describe the probable causes or result. In coordinating with the telephone company to resolve problems and correct circuit deficiencies, they must use a number of terms and phrases which best describe conditions of the waveforms at the terminations. Effective use of this "communications vocabulary" depends on their knowledge and understanding of the many factors concerned with the transmission of intelligence signals, including modulation methods and techniques.

SUMMARY

There are several ways of transforming telephone signals for ease of transmission. They involve imposing the intelligence signals on a higher frequency carrier. When the carrier frequency is varied with the amplitude of the intelligence (modulating) signal, the process is called frequency modulation (FM). When the carrier amplitude is varied with the amplitude of the modulating signal, the process is called amplitude modulation (AM). When one of the sidebands generated in the AM process is filtered from the modulated signal, and the carrier itself is eliminated, the resulting signal is called a single-sideband (SSB) signal. Both AM and FM are used in data-communications systems. Digital signals from EDP machines are often transferred by a technique involving FM; this technique transforms the d.c. levels of a digital signal into different carrier frequencies.

QUESTIONS

Answers to the following questions are listed in Appendix III.

1. What is a "carrier" in the electronic sense?

2. What usually happens to the carrier after the modulated waveform is demodulated?

3. Which four modulation methods are described in this section?

4. What part of an AM waveform represents the original modulating waveform?

5. What four frequencies are present in the composite output waveform from a nonlinear mixer?

6. What part of an FM waveform represents the original modulating waveform?

7. Why does FM transmission produce more realistic sound than AM transmission?

8. What is the main disadvantage of FM compared to AM transmission?

9. How can a single-sideband signal be generated from an AM waveform?

10. What are the advantages of SSB transmission compared to AM transmission?

11. Draw the d.c. data waveform as it would appear at the MODEM data input terminal which would cause the FSK waveform shown below.

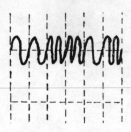

12. The higher frequency in the FSK waveform is called the _____ frequency.

13. During periods of time when data is not being transmitted the MODEM usually remains locked in the _____ condition.

14. If 1200 and 2200 Hz are used as the FSK frequencies, what is the center frequency of the FSK waveform and what is its bandwidth requirement?

15. Why is a single oscillator usually used in FSK generation rather than two separate oscillators?

16. What is the function of the demodulator section of the MODEM?

17. List the advantage of converting d.c. data levels to FSK signals for transmission through telephone circuits.

G Basic Carrier Systems

Telephone companies routinely combine several voice channels for transmission within toll networks. These companies pioneered investigations in search of new techniques to allow simultaneous transmission of two separate conversations over the same pair of wires. Eventually they achieved this, and more. Today, many conversations can pass through the same transmission medium at one time, regardless of whether it is a radio or wired circuit.

The result has been a reduction in the cost of constructing new facilities and more efficient and economical use of existing facilities. Individual subscribers receive better service at lower cost, and a greater number of subscribers are receiving service because of the increased number of channels which are available.

The equipment which is used in telephone circuits to combine voice channels is called "carrier terminal equipment." The process of combining channels is called "multiplexing." Remote carrier equipment is used to "demultiplex" (separate) the channels after transmission is complete.

Carrier terminal equipment is located at either toll switchboards or central offices. Figure G-1 illustrates the basic concept of combining information channels using carrier equipment.

Two major methods of multiplexing information channels are in use. These are called frequency-division multiplexing (FDM) and time-division multiplexing (TDM). TDM is generally used only in undersea cables, and possibly for communications via satellite. FDM is the more common method.

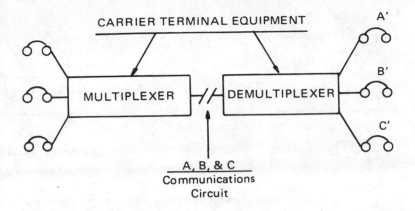

Fig. G-1   A basic multiplex system

TIME DIVISION MULTIPLEXING

The time-division multiplexing process is illustrated in figure G-2. The intelligence signal "A," composed of the elements "aaa..." is being transferred to point A'. The intelligence signal "B," composed of the elements "bbb..." is being transferred to point B'. The TDM technique divides each intelligence signal into small, finite increments of time, and alternately sends a part of each through the circuit. The demultiplexer is synchronized in time to the sending apparatus and alternately applies each received part of each intelligence signal to separate wires.

A normal TDM system "samples" each intelligence waveform at a high rate and reconstructs the waveform through a filtering process at the demultiplexer. Suppose the intelligence signal "A" is divided into 100 samples. During the time that a sample of "B" is applied to the circuit, the corresponding sample of "A" is ignored. Only half of the total samples of each intelligence signal are transmitted.

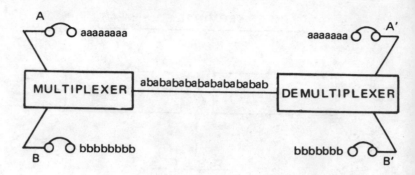

Fig. G-2 Time-division multiplexing and demultiplexing

FREQUENCY DIVISION MULTIPLEXING

Frequency-division multiplexed signals are not susceptible to the distortion found in TDM signals. This is the main reason that FDM systems are more common than TDM systems.

In frequency-division multiplexing, a band of frequencies (a channel) is placed in a different location in the frequency spectrum. This channel is then combined with others which have been transposed to different locations in the frequency spectrum. The combined channels are transmitted through a communications circuit and are separated by a frequency-division demultiplexer at the other end of the circuit. Demultiplexing is accomplished by a reverse process, one which separates and transposes the multiplexed signals back to their original location in the frequency spectrum.

Figure G-3 shows an oscillator-mixer circuit which produces the sum, difference, and original frequencies by heterodyning (nonlinear mixing). The output signals are applied to a bandpass filter which selects only the sum frequencies between 8200 Hz and 11 200 Hz. The operation is identical to generation of upper-sideband signals, except that the 8000 Hz carrier is not an AM or FM radio frequency.

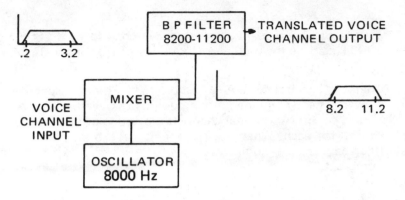

Fig. G-3   Changing the location of an information channel

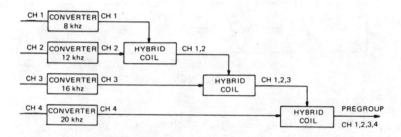

Fig. G-4   Generating the four channels of a pregroup

Voice channels can be transposed to any other location in the frequency spectrum by using appropriate oscillator frequencies and bandpass filters. When two or more voice channels have been transposed to different locations in the frequency spectrum, all that remains to frequency division multiplexing of channels is combining them in such a manner that they do not interfere with each other. This is accomplished using special *linear* mixing devices called "hybrid coils." Hybrid coils combine the transposed voice channel frequencies without heterodyning.

In figure G-4 the oscillator, mixer, and bandpass filters have been combined into one block for each channel. This combination of circuits is called a converter. Each converter produces a USB channel. Each USB channel occupies a section of the frequency spectrum which is located 200 to 3200 Hz above the oscillator frequency of that channel.

Channels 1 and 2 are transposed by their respective converters and combined into a composite waveform by the hybrid circuit. Additional channels are added using a hybrid circuit for each. When four channels have been added in this manner, the composite waveform is referred to as a "pregroup."

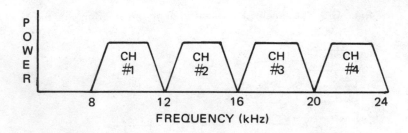

Fig. G-5   Location of channels in a pregroup

Figure G-5 shows the location of the four channels of the pregroup in the frequency spectrum. The pregroup occupies a bandwidth of 16 kHz, a bandpass from 8 to 24 kHz. The information in each channel is separate from intelligence signals in the other channels because it is located in a different part of the spectrum. When the channels are combined by the hybrid circuits, sum and difference frequencies which may interfere with adjacent channels are not produced.

GROUPS, SUPERGROUPS, AND MASTERGROUPS

The process of transposing a band of frequencies to a new location in the spectrum is called "frequency translation." The translated channels are combined by multiplexing. It is common practice to further multiplex three pregroups as shown in figure G-6. Each of the three pregroups is frequency-translated to a different location. The combination of the 12 channels is called a "group" and is composed of three separate pregroups containing four channels each.

The 12 channels of a group occupy a bandwidth of 48 kHz, a bandpass from 60 to 108 kHz. The carrier frequencies of the individual channels are separated from adjacent carriers by 4 kHz. A 3-kHz voice channel occupies part of the frequency spectrum between the carrier frequency locations. In multiplexing of the pregroups, the carrier frequencies and bandpass filters are designed to select the lower sideband intelligence signals. Whether upper or lower sideband systems are used depends on the particular manufacturer's design of the carrier system; it usually does not matter which are used, so long as the same carrier frequencies and sidebands are used in the demultiplexing process.

Individual channels are translated and combined to form larger bands of frequencies called pregroups. Three of the pregroups are further translated (as units) and combined to form groups. In another multiplexing step, the carrier terminal equipment combines five groups into a "supergroup." Each supergroup is composed of 60 voice channels. The final multiplexing step combines 10 supergroups of 60 channels each into a "mastergroup." Each step of the multiplexing process uses appropriate carrier frequencies and bandpass filters which position the total of 600 channels, each at the desired location in the frequency spectrum. A mastergroup (600 channels) is composed of 10 supergroups (60 channels each), which in turn are made up of five groups (12 channels each). Each group is composed of three pregroups (four channels each). Figure G-7 shows the relationship in each step of the multiplexing process. Note that the frequency scale is different in each part of the diagram.

Several companies manufacture carrier terminal equipment. A few of these are Western Electric, Collins Radio, General Electric, and Lenkurt. The carrier frequencies, sideband-selection filters, number of channels per

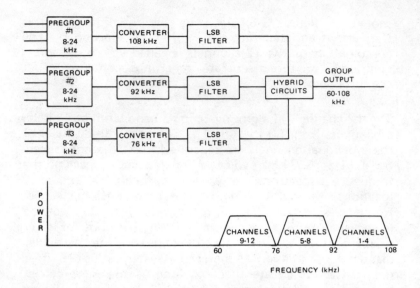

Fig. G-6 Forming a group

multiplexing step and terminology (groups, etc.) varies with manufacturer, but the end result of the processes is similar. Each combines a number of channels for transmission, and separates the channels before they are applied to the receiving subscribers' lines. The examples used here to illustrate frequency-division multiplexing of channels into mastergroups are similar to frequency allocations in Lenkurt Type 46 carrier equipment.

The demultiplexing process is the reverse of that used to combine channels. Appropriate carrier signals are heterodyned with the composite signals. Bandpass filters select the desired sidebands, rejecting all other frequencies. Each step of the demultiplexing process produces the corresponding supergroups, groups, pregroups, and finally the 600 individual channels, each on a separate pair of

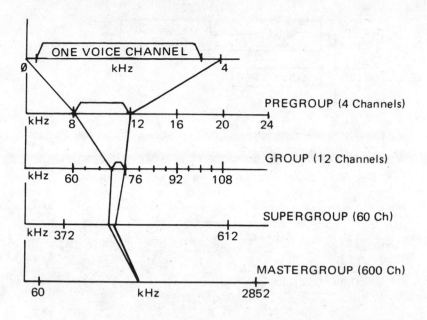

Fig. G-7   Locating one channel in a mastergroup

wires. Figure G-8 through G-11 show the steps in demultiplexing the mastergroup into original form.

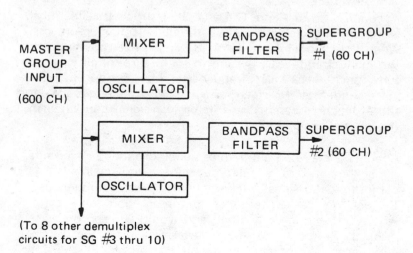

(To 8 other demultiplex circuits for SG #3 thru 10)

Fig. G-8   Demultiplexing a mastergroup into supergroups

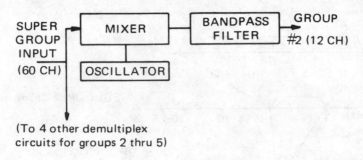

(To 4 other demultiplex
circuits for groups 2 thru 5)

Fig. G-9   Demultiplexing a supergroup into groups

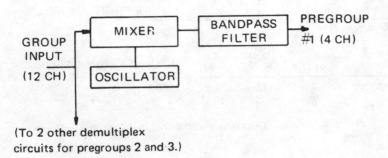

(To 2 other demultiplex
circuits for pregroups 2 and 3.)

Fig. G-10   Demultiplexing a group into pregroups

A comparison of figure G-4 and G-11 shows that identical carrier frequencies are used in the demultiplexing process. When the channel 1 oscillator (8 kHz) is heterodyned with the many frequencies present in the pregroup, all possible sum and difference frequencies are produced. The voice-band filter restricts passage of all frequencies except those which represent the intelligence signal contained in the original channel 1.

Channel 1 may contain a voice signal, channel 2 a facsimile signal, channel 3 a teletype signal, and channel 4 a computer-data signal. These would pass simultaneously through the carrier terminal equipment and toll systems without affecting each other, and would be reproduced in original form at the output terminals of the carrier equipment. Automatic switching equipment at the toll switchboards and central offices at each end of the circuit ensures that the individual channels are correctly connected to their respective terminations.

If the carrier terminal equipment provides 600 channels, all of the channels are present all of the time, whether they are in use or not. All 600 will not be busy at the same time unless the message traffic volume reaches 600 simultaneous calls. The next caller will then hear a signal which means that the trunk is busy.

A telephone circuit may be composed of several types of transmission mediums. Each type of transmission medium has a limited bandwidth, and therefore the number of channels which can be applied is limited. The table in figure

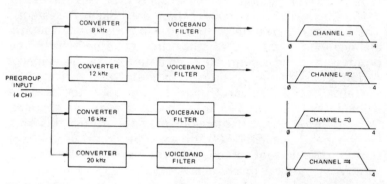

Fig. G-11   Demultiplexing a pregroup into original voice channels

G-12 lists the maximum number of voice frequency channels per carrier system in some of the transmission mediums.

This explanation of carrier terminal equipment has purposely ignored a number of circuits and circuit functions, such as dialing and ringing circuits and signals, subscriber and trunk busy signals, and special circuits which maintain correct operating levels and frequency stability of the signals.

TYPE OF FACILITY	MAXIMUM VOICE CHANNEL CAPACITY
Microwave radio circuits	1800
Coaxial cables	1800
Undersea cables	128
4 wire multiconductor toll cables	24
Open wire overhead lines	16
VHF radio links	12

Fig. G-12   Carrier system capabilities

SYSTEMS USING THE PUBLIC SWITCHED NETWORK

A new variety of business machines is intended for use in the public switched network; these are "dial-up" systems. These systems operate with either manual or automatic dialing which establishes the circuit, after which the business machine is connected and data transfer takes place. Automatic switching equipment at the central offices does not always apply signals from the same point to the same trunk line. It is switched into the next available channel. Depending on the instantaneous message traffic, this may be channel 1, channel 600, or any one in between. As a result, 100-percent predictable results using the dial-up variety of business machine are impossible. A poor-quality channel may be used, one which is not acceptable for data transmission. On the other hand, a different trunk line which is completely acceptable may be used.

Another problem in transmission of data is caused by variation in the quality of the multiplexing circuits. Signals in the carrier-equipment channels do not usually interfere with each other. But an absolute perfect filter has not been constructed, and spurious mixer products are not completely eliminated by the filters. These unwanted signals do interfere with other channels to some degree. The amount of interference depends on such variables as circuit design, age of the electrical components, amplitude of the various intelligence signals, and even to some extent of fluctuations in a.c. and d.c. voltages supplying carrier equipment. Therefore many factors affect the predictability of channel quality, and any of these factors may cause problems with data transmission.

SUMMARY

Two common multiplexing techniques are used. These are called *time-division multiplexing* and *frequency-division multiplexing*.

When information signals are time-division multiplexed, the signals are divided in time. Samples of each signal are transmitted through the circuit, and the intelligence waveforms are reconstructed after transmission. This process has limited applications because of distortion inherent in the process.

When information signals are frequency-division multiplexed, they are translated to new locations in the frequency spectrum. The channels are combined in special hybrid circuits to prevent the generation of heterodyne products which mixers normally produce. The composite waveforms which are transmitted through toll network contain many different intelligence signals. The channels are separated by demultiplexing, a reverse of the multiplexing process.

QUESTIONS

Answers to the following questions are listed in Appendix III.

1. Explain the meaning of the term "multiplexing."

2. Which two multiplexing techniques are used in telephone circuits?

3. Where is carrier terminal equipment located in the telephone systems?

4. What functions does carrier terminal equipment perform?

5. List three circuits required in frequency translation?

6. Why are hybrid coils used in combining translated channels?

7. Why must the frequency-division demultiplexing process use the same carrier frequencies used in the multiplexing process?

8. Describe the function of bandpass filters in a frequency-division multiplex system.

9. What equipment is responsible for ensuring that individual channels of a carrier system are correctly connected to the respective terminations?

10. Why is there a limit to the maximum number of channels which may be applied to a given transmission medium when the channels are frequency-division multiplexed?

11. Is it possible to combine as many as 1800 voice channels in one transmission medium?

Basic Characteristics of a Wire Transmission Line

The simplest communications channel is composed of two wires. It is an electrical circuit through which signals are transferred. In most applications, wire is considered as a near perfect conductor. Wire characteristics are negligible. However, in communications circuits these characteristics must be considered.

When the length of a transmission line is increased, an appreciable amount, the characteristics become significant because they directly affect channel quality. They must be considered in obtaining satisfactory communication through the channel.

The three basic characteristics of wire transmission lines are resistance, reactance, and impedance.

RESISTANCE

Every conductor, insulator, or material thing exhibits some quantity of resistance to the flow of electrical currents. A voltage or electromotive force is necessary to overcome the resistance and force current to flow. When this happens, current flow through the resistance produces heat. The amount of heat is called power and is expressed in watts. Voltage and power divide in a series circuit according to the ratio of resistances.

In long transmission lines, resistance of the wire becomes an appreciable amount of the total resistance of a series circuit. Power developed by line resistance is lost as far as output power is concerned. In figure H-1, a wire which has a resistance of 5 ohms per mile is used to connect a 100-volt battery to 10 different 100-watt light bulbs located 1 mile from the source. Since the total length of wire used is 2 miles, total line resistance equals 10 ohms.

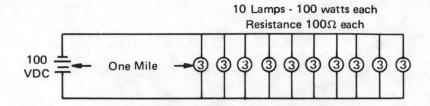

Fig. H-1 Example of line resistance effect

Simple electronic formulas show that 500 watts of total power is developed in the circuit. Half of the total power, 250 watts, is developed by wire resistance and is wasted. The remaining 250 watts is divided among the 10 lamp circuits; each lamp therefore develops only 25 watts of power, instead of the intended 100 watts.

Wire resistance depends on several factors. One of them is the material or metal which is used to construct the conductor. Table H-1 lists the resistance of some metals compared to copper. Copper is most commonly used, is accepted as the standard for comparison, and has a relative resistance of one (1). Steel wire, which might be necessary because of higher tensile strength, results in more power loss than copper wire of the same dimensions.

Length and diameter of wires also affects total power losses. If cross-sectional area of a given length of wire is increased,the resistance is lowered. On the other hand, if diameter is held constant and length is increased, the total resistance will increase a proportional amount. For example, if 1 mile of wire has 3 ohms of resistance, 5 miles of the same wire will have 15 ohms of resistance. The Appendix I contains a table of wire resistances and current capacities for standard American Wire Gauge (AWG) dimensions of copper wire.

As the frequency of a.c. signals applied to a wire is increased, current tends to flow nearer the surface, away from the physical center of the wire. Since less of the cross-sectional area is used, the effective resistance of the wire increases in proportion to increases in frequency. This

Conductor	Relative Resistance
Silver	0.92
Gold	1.38
Aluminum	1.59
Steel	8.62

Table H-1   Relative resistance of common metals

phenomenon is called "skin effect" and becomes important in carrier systems.

Resistance of wire is usually measured per unit length, for example, ohms per thousand feet, kilometer, mile or loop mile. A loop mile is a term which describes two wires connecting two points which are physically located one mile apart.

Table H-2 lists the resistance per unit length of some common wire sizes used in U.S. telephone systems.

Even the relatively short lines (a few thousand feet) may have enough series resistance to cause marginal circuit operation, particularly if the wire is very small in diameter. Small diameter wires can also be a safety hazard. If the current-carrying capacity of a wire is exceeded, it may develop enough heat to start fires or even to destroy the wire.

REACTANCE

A second property of two wire lines which is important in communications circuits is reactance. Reactance is symbolized by "X" and is a measure of opposition to the flow of alternating currents. The amount of reactance is expressed in ohms. The two types of reactance are those caused by inductors (inductive reactance or X_l) and capacitors (capacitive reactance or X_c).

Circuit Type	AWG	Diameter (mm)	Resistance (Ω) 1000'	Loop Mile
Subscriber line	22	1.0	16	
Subscriber line	24	.79	25	
Subscriber line	26	.625	40	
Toll wire	19	1.42	8	
Interoffice wire	19	1.42	8	
Open wire lines				
(copper)	10	4		6.7
(copper)	12	3		10.2
(copper clad steel)	12	3		25
(copper clad steel)	14	2		44

Table H-2   Telephone wire sizes and resistances

All wires, regardless of length, have some inductance. It is considered to be in series with the wire and to increase in proportion to wire length. Beyond a certain length, transmission line can be divided into "line segments" or "sections," each composed of a fixed amount of inductance, and each identical to all other sections in that line. This is schematically shown in figure H-2.

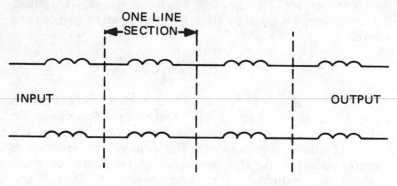

Fig. H-2   Representation of inductance in line sections

The formula for inductive reactance is

$$X_l = 2\pi f L$$

where 2π is a constant, f is frequency, and L is inductance in henries. A graph of X_l plotted against frequency for a fixed inductor may appear as shown in figure H-3.

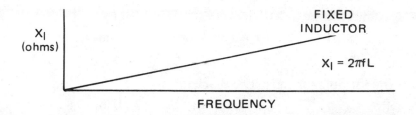

Fig. H-3   Graphing inductive reactance

In the graph, opposition to current flow (X_l) increases as frequency is increased. Suppose a fixed amplitude a.c. signal is applied to the long transmission line in figure H-2, and then the frequency of the signal is steadily increased while the amplitude is held constant. Increasing the frequency causes an increased inductive reactance, effectively reducing the amplitude or voltage of the output signal. When high frequency signals are applied, losses occur in the transmission line because of its inherent self-inductance.

All wires also have a certain amount of capacitance between them. This capacitance produces capacitive reactance. A capacitor is defined as two conductors which are separated by a dielectric material, and the transmission line is two conductors separated by a dielectric material. As shown in figure H-4, a circuit may be divided into line sections containing fixed amounts of capacitance. From the diagram, the capacitors representing each line section are between the wires and are parallel with each other.

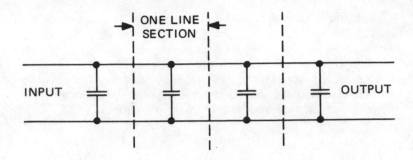

Fig. H-4   Representation of capacitance in line sections

The formula for capacitive reactance is

$$X_c = \frac{1}{2\pi fC}$$

where 2π is again a constant, f is frequency, and C is capacitance in farads. A graph which plots X_c against frequency appears in figure H-5. Capacitance does not vary.

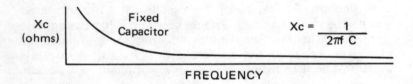

Fig. H-5   Graphing capacitive reactance

The curve in figure H-5 is nonlinear. As frequency increases, the capacitors approach a short circuit condition. Opposition to current flow decreases with increasing frequency, but the formula and graph indicate that current flow is *not* in series with the wires. Rather, it is *between* them. The result is similar to the effect which inductive reactance causes. Higher frequency signals are reduced in amplitude at the output terminals. But this time it is a reduction of X_c tending to short out more of the signals, which causes the reduction in amplitude.

"Line losses" (wasted power) occur at all frequencies in a transmission line because of wire resistance, and line losses increase as higher frequencies are transmitted through the circuit because of the wire reactances. The latter effect is called "poor high frequency response" and is a significant consideration where any long transmission line is concerned.

IMPEDANCE

Impedance is a third important characteristic of wired lines. Impedance is a number which is symbolized by the letter "Z" and is expressed in ohms. It *is a combination* of the resistance and reactance factors which are a part of any transmission line and is given by the following formula:

$$Z = \sqrt{R^2 + (X_l - X_c)^2}$$

where R is line section resistance and X indicates respective reactances. Figure H-6 is a schematic representation of a inductive and capacative transmission line showing the elements which contribute to line impedance.

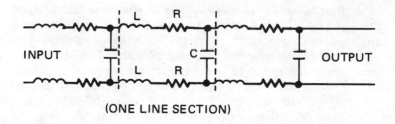

(ONE LINE SECTION)

Fig. H-6   Impedance factors of wired transmission lines

Study of the formula and diagram can lead to some interesting conclusions about transmission line impedance. For example, suppose X_l equals X_c. From the formula, the line impedance (Z) is equal to line resistance (R). Therefore, the *minimum* impedance of any transmission line section *must* be equal to resistance of that line section.

Any difference between X_l and X_c must result in Z being greater than R.

Further study of the formula reveals that Z must be frequency, dependent. Since the value of Z depends in part on X_l and X_c, and since each of these varies with frequency, impedance of a transmission line must also vary with frequency. If the resistance, inductance, and capacitance values of a particular cable pair (two wires of a multiconductor cable) are known, a graph plotting impedance against frequency may be constructed, producing a curve similar to that shown in figure H-7.

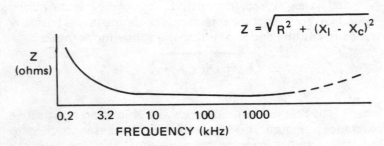

$$Z = \sqrt{R^2 + (X_l - X_c)^2}$$

Fig. H-7   Typical impedance/frequency curve for cable

Line impedance varies more widely in the voice band region than at higher frequencies. The impedance of the line varies a considerable amount *within* the voice band. It should be obvious that any *statement* of transmission line impedance must be in *reference* to some particular frequency. To say that a transmission line has 600 ohms of impedance does not really describe conditions at all voice frequencies. A more accurate description gives the impedance as "600 ohms at 1000 Hz," since this description defines a particular operating point or characteristic of the line.

Transmission line impedances within telephone company circuits vary widely. Overhead open-wire lines, multiconductor cables, and coaxial cables each exhibit different impedances to the a.c. signals. However, impedance of the subscriber lines which connect to the termination points has been standardized at 500, 600, or 1000 ohms when the reference frequency is 1000 Hz. For reasons which become clear later, *600 ohms at 1000 Hz* is almost universally accepted as the standard.

Different types of lines have different impedances. Wire resistance depends on length, diameter, and material used in construction of the wire. Inductance is that property of conductors which tends to oppose any change in the existing magnetic field around the wire, and which depends on such variables as wire size, shape, amount of instantaneous current flow, and proximity to other conductors. Capacitance is also a variable and depends on total size of the conductors, relative size in respect to each other, spacing between conductors, and type of dielectric material which separates them. In view of this, it should be clear that transmission line impedances differ between coaxial cables, multiconductor cables and open-wire overhead lines. Even wired circuits which use the same gauge and length of wire will have different impedances if the spacing between wires of each pair is not the same.

A theoretical line is divided into segments in which each is identical to every other segment of the line. If the impedance of one line section is fixed, then it follows that the impedance of the line will be constant regardless of the number of sections in the line or which point on the wires is used as a reference for measurements. If a cable pair is designed for 600-ohm use, then it exhibits a 600-ohm impedance to input and output terminations, as well as at any other point along the line.

IMPEDANCE MATCHING

Subscribers have equipment which physically and electrically connects to the terminations of telephone lines, or perhaps to lengthy "in-house" circuits which do not belong to the telephone company. Input and output circuits in various units of equipment also have characteristic impedances, and whether these are resistive or reactive does not usually matter. It is the amount of impedance that is important. Transmission line impedances cannot be considered unless the line is properly terminated. That is, the line must have the correct impedances connected to input and output terminations to ensure sufficient signal transmission.

In most cases, one of the transmission objectives is to transfer signals through the transmission line with minimum power loss. Maximum power transfer occurs when impedances are matched. Transmission lines have maximum efficiency and minimum power loss when input and output impedances are equal, and when the transmission line has been designed for these impedances. When equipment is connected to transmission lines, the technician should ensure that the lines are properly terminated, and he should recognize that a reduction in signal amplitude at the output terminals of the line may be caused by mismatching the impedances.

Perhaps the best way to illustrate the importance of impedance matching for power transfer is by using another example. Assume that there is a theoretically perfect transmission line (one which has no losses). The following example illustrates the effect of purposely mismatching impedances and shows what happens to power at the output termination. The example is valid for d.c. voltages, and the same effect holds true for a.c. signals. Figure H-8 shows a hypothetical circuit when it is impedance-matched. The source and termination impedances are 600 ohms.

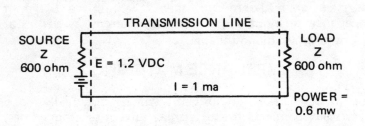

Fig.   H-8   Impedance matched circuit

If the battery voltage is 1.2 volts, a current of 1 ma flows, and power delivered to the load resistance is 0.6 milliwatts. If the load impedance is mismatched by 50 percent, calculations shows a change in power delivered to the load resistor. The diagram for both cases (increase and decrease) is shown in figure H-9.

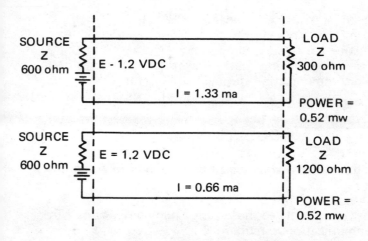

Fig. H-9   Intentional mismatched impedances

Power delivered to the load circuit is 0.6 milliwatts when the circuit is impedance matched. Only 0.52 milliwatts of power is delivered to the load circuit with a 50 percent impedance mismatch. This represents a loss or waste of 13 percent of the power. The 13-percent loss may be enough to make the difference between marginal and acceptable circuit operation.

Now that the importance of proper terminations and impedance matching is clear, consider the nonlinear impedances which transmission lines present to varying-frequency a.c. signals. Impedance matching is much more critical when bands of frequencies are concerned. A circuit which is properly impedance matched at 3200 Hz is not impedance matched at 200 Hz because impedance of the transmission line changes. This is one of the main reasons why 1000 Hz is selected as the reference frequency. Impedance of ordinary cable using number 22 AWG wire varies from 1288 ohms at 200 Hz to approximately 300 ohms at 3200 Hz. At 1000 Hz this cable typically has 580 ohms of impedance.

SUMMARY

Resistance, reactance, and impedance are characteristics of wire transmission lines. Losses within lines caused by these characteristics are very important factors in signal attenuation; minimizing such losses is necessary for acceptable communication through wire circuits.

QUESTIONS

Answers to the following questions are listed in Appendix III.

1. What are the three most basic characteristics of wire communications circuits?

2. Which characteristic of a wire transmission line is responsible for power loss (dissipation) in that line?

3. What factors affect the resistance of a wired line?

4. What is "skin effect"?

5. Which material is accepted as the standard for comparison of the relative resistance of metals?

6. What is the approximate resistance of a 4000-foot, two-wire line of 26 AWG dimensions as measured at one end if the remote ends of the wires are shorted together?

7. As applied frequency increases, the inductive reactance of a wire line _____ and the capacitive reactance of the line _____ .

8. The series inductance and shunt capacitance of a wired transmission line cause the pair of wires to act similar to a filter. The effect of these reactances causes poor _____ frequency response.

9. Impedance (Z) of a transmission line depends upon _____ , _____ , and _____ of the line.

10. Why is transmission line impedance specified as "600 ohms at 1000 Hz" rather than as just 600 ohms?

11. Why must the equipment connected to each end of a telephone circuit be a specific value of impedance?

The Decibel, a Ratio of Powers

The terms volts, ohms, amperes, watts, frequency, and time all designate positive quantities that can be analyzed and interpreted. But the meaning of the term "decibel" seems to elude many electronics technicians, particularly when they are employed in specialized fields such as EDP.

The most probable factors which contribute to the mystery surrounding the decibel are that the decibel does not represent any value *by itself*, and that as a unit it is not on a linear scale. But there is no real mystery. "Decibel" is a highly versatile and appropriate term which often best describes a.c. power gains and losses. The decibel is a comparison, not a measurement. When a reference point is stated, the decibel has concrete value and can be used in similar context to other electronics terms. The decibel has been adopted by telephone companies and other communications agencies as an expression of power gain and loss.

BELS

Early experiments with sound and hearing revealed that we do not hear sounds on a linear scale. A sound increased to twice its former power level does not sound twice as loud. As a matter of fact, the change is barely perceptible. They searched for a unit of measure which would more closely approximate the response of the human ear. The unit which gained acceptance was the bel, named after Alexander Graham Bell.

The bel is simply a ratio of two power levels, one of which is 10 times as great as the other. It applies equally well to sound power levels in the atmosphere, vibrations in an airplane wing, or signal power levels in an electronic circuit.

The term bel is a relative term, like "rich," "poor," "up," and "down." These do not have meaning unless some reference point is stated. In communications circuits, power levels at circuit input terminals serve as a reference. Input power levels are considered to be "zero bels," and output power levels are described as a number of bels of gain or loss compared to this reference. When the circuit has *gain* the ratio is positive, and when power *losses* occur the ratio is negative. Table I-1 illustrates the relationship between bel units, power ratios, and power gains and losses.

POLARITY	BELS	RATIO (1:)	CHANGE
	4	10000	
Positive	3	1000	GAIN
	2	100	
	1	10	
NONE– – – – – – –	–0– – – – – – –	– 1– – – – – –	– EQUAL
	1	0.1	
	2	0.01	
Negative	3	0.001	LOSS
	4	0.0001 ·	

Table   I-1   Bels as power ratios = gains and losses

The main advantage of expressing gains and losses in bels (as ratios) is that large ratios can be expressed in simple form. For example, when we say that a circuit has a power gain of 8 bels, we mean that output power from the circuit is one-hundred million (100 000 000) times greater than input power to the circuit.

In practice, the bel is too large a unit for many applications. In addition it is difficult to accurately define some ratios of power gains and losses. A ratio of 50 000 is between 4 and 5 bels, but the range between 4 and 5 bels is so great that the description is not very accurate. In practice the bel is divided into ten parts, called decibels, permitting greater accuracy in expressions of power ratios.

The system of bels is a linear progression (1,2,3...), but the ratios which they represent are not linear (1,10,100,1000...). A ratio of zero bels indicates equal input and output power levels. A 1-bel gain means that output power is 10 times as great as input power, and a 2-bel gain means that output power is 100 times as great as input power. Figure I-1 illustrates a continuation of this nonlinear relationship. A 5-watt reference input signal is applied to the circuit input terminals. The graph is produced by assuming the circuit gain to be adjustable, and plotting the absolute power level of the output signal versus the ratio of power gain. At 1-bel of gain, the output power is 50 watts. The output power is 500 watts at 2 bels of gain, 5000 watts at 3 bels of gain, and so on. Obviously, a change of power level at the output terminals from 0 to 1 bel (a 45-watt change) is not equal to the change from 1 to 2 bels (a 450-watt change).

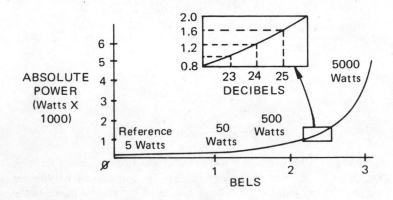

Fig. I-1   Gain in power and db

The shape of the line in figure I-1 is called a logarithmic curve. The insert illustrates that the bel is *not* divided into 10 *equal* parts. If the curve were linear, 25 decibels would equal half the difference between 2- and 3-bels, or 2250 watts. However, based upon the 5-watt reference, 25 decibels equals an absolute power level at the output terminals of only 1600 watts.

Expressions of power gains and losses in bels or decibels are ratios and must be in respect to some specified reference to be meaningful. A power gain of 25 decibels based on a 5-watt reference means that there is 1600 watts of power at the circuit output terminals. A different refrence input-power level causes a different output-power level, even though the circuit gain may still be expressed as 25 decibels.

Since the nature of the expressions is logarithmic, a nonlinear or logarithmic system of mathematics must be used in the computations of circuit power gains and losses in decibels. A brief description of relevant formulas and mathematics follows for those who are inclined toward proofs and conversions.

The formulas for solving gain or loss in decibels are listed below. These are only valid if the impedance at the points of measurement (input and output terminals) is the same. Tables for referencing gain and loss figures directly are included later in the section.

$$db = 10 \log_{10} (P\text{-}1/P\text{-}2)$$
$$= 20 \log_{10} (E\text{-}1/E\text{-}2)$$
$$= 20 \log_{10} (I\text{-}1/I\text{-}2)$$

In the formula, db is the number of decibels of gain or loss, $\log_{10}$ is the common (base 10) logarithm of the ratio, and (P-1/P-2), (E-1/E-2), and (I-1/I-2) are the ratios of measured input and output levels in terms of *power*, *voltage*, or *current*. P-1, E-1, or I-1 are the circuit output levels, and P-2, E-2, or I-2 are the circuit input values. If the ratio is positive (for example, P-1 is greater than P-2), the number of decibels represents the ratio of power gain. Conversely, if the ratio is negative (for example, P-1 is less than P-2), the number of decibels represents the ratio of power loss.

LOGARITHMIC NOTATION

The logarithm of a quantity is the exponent of the power to which a given number, called the base, must be raised in order to equal the quantity. This is illustrated in the following examples.

a. $10^3 = 1000$
   $3 = \log 1000$ to the base 10

b. $10^4 = 10000$
   $4 = \log 10000$ to the base 10

c. $a^x = b$

   $X = \log$ of b to the base a

Many systems of logarithms are possible, since any number may be used as the base. In the base-10, or *common,* log system, the logarithms of integral powers of 10 are positive or negative whole numbers, as illustrated in table I-2.

POWERS OF 10	LOGARITHMIC NOTATION
$10^3 = 1{,}000$	$\log_{10} 1{,}000 = 3$
$10^2 = 100$	$\log_{10} 100 = 2$
$10^1 = 10$	$\log_{10} 10 = 1$
$10^{-1} = 0.1$	$\log_{10} 0.1 = -1$
$10^{-2} = 0.01$	$\log_{10} 0.01 = -2$
$10^{-3} = 0.001$	$\log_{10} 0.0001 = -3$

Table I-2   Logarithms related to powers of 10

The logarithm of a number which is not an integral power of 10 consists of a whole number and a decimal fraction. The integral part of the logarithm is called the "characteristic," and the decimal part is called the "mantissa."

In solving the decibel formula, the ratio of input and output levels is first calculated. The logarithm of the ratio, which is multiplied by either 10 or 20 (depending on whether the measurements were made in watts, volts, or amperes) is found to complete the calculation. The method of determining the base-10 logarithm of the ratio is explained below.

DETERMINING THE LOGARITHM OF A NUMBER

a.   *Determining the characteristic* - There are two rules for determining the characteristic of a logarithm:

(1)   If the number (ratio) is greater than *one,* the characteristic is one less than the number of digits to the left of the decimal point.

(a)   The characteristic of 1600 is three (3).

(b)   The characteristic of 1.6 is zero (0).

(2)   If the number (ratio) is less than *one,* the characteristic is negative, and is one more than the number of zeroes to the right of the decimal point.

The mantissa of a logarithm is always positive. In order to maintain the complete logarithm positive, the characteristic is written as a positive number minus 10.

(a)   The characteristic of 0.25 is -1 (or 9 - 10).

(b)   The characteristic of 0.0666 is -2 (or 8 - 10).

(c)   The characteristic of 0.000005423 is -6 (or 4 - 10).

b.   *Determining the mantissa* - The mantissa (decimal part) of the logarithm is determined using tables which have been compiled to the correct base. The first three digits of the number (ratio) identify a row and column in the table. The sequence of digits at the point of intersection of that row and column is the mantissa of the logarithm. A table of common, base-10, logarithms is located in appendix I, and has been used to compute the logarithm of the numbers in the preceeding examples. In this application, it is necessary to use only the first three digits of the mantissa, regardless of the number of digits shown in the table.

- The logarithm of 1600 is 3.204

- The logarithm of 1.6 is 0.204

- The logarithm of 0.25 is 9.397 - 10

- The logarithm of 0.0666 is 8.823 - 10

- The logarithm of 0.000005423 is 4.733 - 10

When a circuit has power loss, the ratio is less than one and the characteristic is negative. The simplest approach to this type of problem is to remember that the circuit has power loss, then to solve the ratio as a positive quantity. The larger power level is divided by the smaller power level (regardless of which is input or output). This yields a positive characteristic for use in the formula. After the formula is solved a minus sign (−) is prefixed to the decibel quantity to identify that the expression is power loss rather than power gain.

The hypothetical communications circuit in figure I-2 illustrates a solution in decibels when the power levels are known. The reference input power level is 2 mw, and the output power level from the circuit is 0.005 milliwatt.

| INPUT POWER = 2 mw @ 1000 Hz | COMMUNICATIONS CIRCUIT | OUTPUT POWER = 0.005 mw @ 1000 Hz |

Fig. I-2   Circuit for decibel calculations

PROBLEM: What is the gain or loss in decibels of the circuit shown in figure I-2?

SOLUTION: $db = 10 \log_{10} (P\text{-}1/p\text{-}2)$

$db = 10 \log_{10} (2/0.005)$

$db = 10 \log_{10} (400)$

$db = 10 (2.603)$

$db = -26.03$

Therefore, the circuit has a power gain of -26.03 db, or a power loss of 26.03 db. A 26-db power loss is usually unacceptable for data transmission in a practical telephone circuit.

When the impedances are different at the points of measurement, the decibel formula using power levels is valid. But if the measurements are obtained in voltage or current values, the difference in impedances must be taken into consideration. The formulas to be used when the impedances differ are as follows.

$$db = 20 \log_{10} \frac{E\text{-}1 \sqrt{Z\text{-}2}}{E\text{-}2 \sqrt{Z\text{-}1}}$$

$$db = 20 \log_{10} \frac{I\text{-}1 \sqrt{Z\text{-}1}}{I\text{-}2 \sqrt{Z\text{-}2}}$$

Through the coordinated efforts of many groups of people the situation has been simplified. An arbitrary power level of *one milliwatt* when the circuit impedance is *600 ohm* and the test frequency is *1000 Hz* has been accepted as a standard unit of measure. This unit is called the "dbm," "m" meaning milliwatt. Voltmeters are available which provide readings directly in dbm units.

Several factors affect the accuracy of dbm meters. The main reason for the evolution of dbm meters is standardization of telephone circuit impedances at 600 ohms at the terminations. The readings obtained from a dbm meter are *not* accurate unless the circuit impedance is the same as that for which the meter was designed. Also, there are meters which are designed for other circuit impedances, and which do not provide accurate measurements in 600-ohm circuits. Finally, since circuit impedance varies with frequency, the readings in dbm are not accurate unless the correct reference frequency (usually 1000 Hz) is applied when the measurements are performed.

When the reference is fixed, as it is in dbm, the units have a real value in terms of voltage, current, or power. Zero dbm always means that 1 mw, or 0.775 volts RMS, is developed across the circuit terminals when the test frequency is 1000 Hz and the circuit impedance is 600 ohms. Minus 10 dbm always means that the level is 0.245 volts RMS across the stated impedance, and that the power developed in that impedance is 100 microwatts. Since this direct relationship holds when dbm are used, charts can be constructed listing the values of the corresponding levels. Also, since normal conditions within a communications circuit may result in completely acceptable tolerance levels of 4 or 5 db differences in power gain or loss, the charts serve as a convenient means of approximating the circuit conditions and avoiding lengthy mathematical conversions otherwise required when dbm meters are not available.

Measurements meaningful in EDP communications are confined to a range of 4- or 5-bels (40 or 50 decibels). In a previous example the circuit power loss is 26.03 db. The amount of loss is *probably not* acceptable. The same is true if the loss is 23 db, 25 db, or 28 db. The fact that it is 26.03 db of power loss is not nearly as significant as the fact that the power loss exceeds 20 db.

Telephone circuits which have too much power gain are rare. Transmission problems involving telephone circuits are usually the result of excessive power loss.

Measurements of the signal levels in a circuit, are normally made with an oscilloscope, a dbm meter, or a RMS voltmeter. If a dbm meter is available, the levels may be measured directly in dbm. Oscilloscopes normally display the peak-to-peak values of the waveforms, and most voltmeters are calibrated in RMS or effective values. If an oscilloscope is used for measurements for the decibel formulas, the peak-to-peak value of the waveform must be converted to RMS value. Table I-3 lists the formulas which express the relationships between peak-to-peak and RMS values of a.c. voltages.

$$
\begin{aligned}
\text{peak-to-peak} &= 2 \times \text{peak} \\
\text{peak-to-peak} &= 2.828 \times \text{RMS} \\
\text{peak} &= 0.5 \times \text{peak-to-peak} \\
\text{peak} &= 1.414 \times \text{RMS} \\
\text{RMS} &= 0.707 \times \text{peak} \\
\text{RMS} &= \text{Effective value}
\end{aligned}
$$

Table I-3   Relationship between a-c waveform values

Assuming the standard circuit impedance (600 ohms), reference frequency (1000 Hz), and power level (1 mw), the formulas have been used to construct table I-4, which correlates dbm units, RMS voltages, peak-to-peak voltages, and circuit power levels. The table can be used to approximate power levels to within 3 dbm of accuracy when the circuit voltages are known, or to approximate the circuit voltages when the loss or gain is known in dbm. Note that the table is only valid for the stated conditions. If the telephone company expresses levels in dbm, but normally provides a different termination impedance (for example, 900 ohms), this table is not valid. In this case, the formulas may be used to construct a similar table in which the 900-ohm circuit voltage values correspond to the dbm signal power levels. Once generated, that table is as useful for a situation such as this one is for conversions in 600-ohm circuits. A more detailed version of this table is available in Appendix I.

The left hand column shows gain or loss in dbm units compared to the reference level of 1 mw at 600 ohms. The second column shows equivalent RMS or effective voltages as measured with standard a.c. voltmeters. The third column shows corresponding peak-to-peak voltages displayed on an oscilloscope, and the final column lists the

dbm	RMSV	PPV	POWER	
50	245.0	690	100	Watts (W)
45	138.0	390	31.7	W
40	77.5	220	10.0	W
35	43.5	123	3.17	W
30	24.5	69	1.0	W
25	13.8	39	317.0	Milliwatts (mw)
20	7.75	22	100.0	mw
15	4.35	12	31.7	mw
10	2.45	6.9	10.0	mw
5	1.38	3.9	3.17	mw
0	0.775	2.2	1.00	mw
5	0.435	1.2	317.00	Microwatts (uw)
10	0.245	0.69	100.00	uw
15	0.138	0.39	31.70	uw
20	0.0775	0.22	10.00	uw
25	0.0435	0.12	3.17	uw
30	0.0245	0.069	1.00	uw
35	0.0138	0.039	0.317	uw
40	0.00775	0.022	0.100	uw
45	0.00435	0.012	0.0317	uw
50	0.00245	0.0069	0.0100	uw

Table I-4   Table of equivalence (dbm)

amount of power which these voltages produce in a 600-ohm circuit. All quantities in the table have been rounded off to two or three significant digits because practical measurements do not provide greater accuracy.

Use of the table is an approach which avoids the mathematics, is simple, and provides sufficient accuracy. Suppose a 1000 Hz voltage is measured at 0.02 volts RMS. From the table, the same voltage measured on an oscilloscope is approximately 0.06 volts peak-to-peak, and corresponds to approximately -33 dbm.

One of the advantages of working with dbm units is that these can be added to and subtracted from one another to arrive at conclusions about the circuit operation. For example, if the input power transmit level equals -8 dbm and the output power receive level equals -15 dbm, then the amount of power lost in the circuit equals 7 dbm (15 -8). If the transmit level equals -8 dbm and the receive level equals

-6 dbm, then the circuit gain equals 2 dbm (8 - 6). In this approach the intuitive notion of gain or loss is the simplest method of determining the circuit gain characteristic.

Telephone companies typically require an input-power transmit level to be in the range of 0 dbm to -16 dbm. In return, they usually guarantee to provide output power levels from their circuits which exceed -16 dbm. For the present we will assume this is normal, that the range from -16 dbm to -22 dbm is marginal, and that output power levels below -22 dbm are unacceptable.

DECIBEL CASE STUDIES

The following examples are hypothetical situations intended to show the use of the table I-4, and to illustrate expressions of power levels in dbm units. Suppose two technicians are working with an online system. One is at the central processor, and another is at the remote terminal. The telephone circuit is designed to operate half-duplex, two-wire, and point-to-point. They use the table to make conversions from one signal form to another, and use these approximations to arrive at logical decisions about the circuit. The numbers in parentheses following each use of the table are values which have been calculated using appropriate formulas.

CASE 1

Problem: The technician at the processor transmits a 1-kHz signal at -8 dbm. The remote-terminal is receiving, measured on an oscilloscope, 0.18 volts PP.

Evaluation: The transmit level is adequate. From the table, the remote-terminal receive level is approximately -22 dbm (-21.7 dbm). The circuit has about 15 dbm of power loss (13.7 dbm).

Conclusion: The circuit power loss exceeds specifications and even marginal operation is doubtful. Coordination should be arranged with the telephone company to improve the circuit gain characteristic.

CASE 2

Problem: The remote terminal is transmitting a 1-kHz signal from the terminal; it is measured at 1.5 volts PP on an oscilloscope at the terminal. The processor is receiving 0.3 volts RMS (the dbm meter is broken).

Evaluation: The remote transmit level is approximately -4 dbm (-3.2 dbm). The processor level is approximately -8 dbm (-7.96 dbm). The circuit power loss is approximately 4 dbm (4.76 dbm).

Conclusion: The communications circuit works well. If the error rate in the business machines is excessive, the fault is probably in them rather than in the telephone circuit. Both technicians should prove our equipment is not at fault before contacting the telephone company.

CASE 3

Problem: The system works well when transmitting to the terminal, but incurs a high error rate when receiving from the terminal. The remote terminal transmit level is measured at 0.23 volts RMS, and it is received at -18 dbm (the dbm meter is fixed).

Evaluation: The receive level of -18 dbm is marginal. From the table, his transmit level is approximately -12 dbm (-10.6 dbm). The circuit power loss is approximately 6 dbm (7.2 dbm).

Conclusion: The telephone circuit is providing a marginal output level when the **transmit-power** level is within specifications. But the remote transmit level may be increased without exceeding the input power specification. If the transmit level is adjusted to provide a 4 dbm increase, it should then be received at -14 dbm (each increases a like amount). The error rate should be reduced and the circuit operation satisfactory. The telephone company may still have to be contacted, but the subscriber is probably saved the charge for a telephone-company service call.

SUMMARY

For ease in handling significant changes in signal levels, a logarithmic system of measurement is used. Measurements in gain and loss within a communication system are described *bels* or *decibels*. Computation of significant gain or loss within a circuit is facilitated by tables of logarithms. Special test equipment is available for circuits of standard impedance to measure decibel gain or loss with respect to one milliwatt.

QUESTIONS

Answers to the following questions are listed in Appendix III.

1. How does "bel" describe the relationship between two power levels?

2. A three bel power loss indicates that output power from the circuit is _____ times as much as power input to the circuit.

3. Two bels equal _____ decibels.

4. Why must logarithms be used in decibel computations?

5. What is the logarithm of one million (1,000,000) to the base 10?

6. What are the reference levels at which power in a circuit equals 0 dbm?

7. List the factors affecting the validity of readings obtained with a dbm meter.

8. Oscilloscopes normally display a.c. waveforms in _____ ___ _____ value, and voltmeters are normally calibrated in _____ value of the waveform.

9. If a voltage is measured as 0.4 volts peak-to-peak in a 600-ohm circuit, the equivalent RMS value is approximately _____ volts and the approximate power level is _____ dbm.

10. If the power applied to the input terminals of a telephone circuit is -9 dbm, and the power delivered from the telephone circuit to the receiving equipment is -18 dbm, how much power gain or loss occurs in the telephone circuit?

11. In the preceeding question, if the transmit power level of -9 dbm is increased to -5 dbm, the expected receive level at the remote location is _____ dbm.

J A Survey of Transmission Problems

One of the greatest challenges facing the EDP technician is resolving data-transmission problems in an online system. Correct analysis of the situation and decision on an appropriate course of action, regardless of whether the fault lies in the equipment or the telephone circuit, is the heart of the EDP technician's work.

In the past, the telephone circuit has often been unduly suspected by EDP technicians, resulting in unnecessary service calls by telephone company personnel. This approach is both expensive and inefficient. Each time the telephone company tests the circuit, it imposes a service charge if the circuit is not defective. The EDP technician has no recourse except to begin again, and valuable time has been wasted.

This section describes the more common transmission problems encountered by the online technician. The objectives of this section are to develop an awareness of the problems and their causes, to describe units of measure, and to propose some test methods which support fault-finding technique.

The five major problem areas discussed in this text are attenuation, noise, echoes and reflections, crosstalk, and delay. These problems all coexist in varying degrees in *every* communications circuit. When a telephone circuit provides marginal operation, it is usually attributable to more than one of these factors, but correcting for the most prominent factor usually restores the circuit to an acceptable level of quality.

ATTENUATION

Attenuation is a term which applies to the amplitude of the signals which are transmitted. It usually implies a reduction in amplitude of one or more of the elements of the intelligence waveform. Three distinct catagories of amplitude changes are: attenuation, attenuation distortion, and attenuation frequency distortion.

The single word *attenuation* usually means that all frequencies under consideration are equally affected. The major cause of attenuation, line resistance, has been described in section H. Attenuation may also be caused by failure of amplifier circuits, high resistance or open wires, current leakage between wires, or wet cables. The amount of attenuation can be expressed in terms of voltage, current, power, or dbm. In telephone circuits it is more common to use dbm.

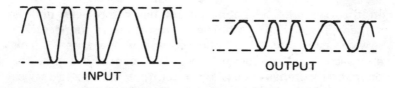

INPUT

OUTPUT

Fig.   J-1   Effect of attenuation on FSK waveforms

Suppose a MODEM is conditioned to apply the mark frequency (1200 Hz) to the transmission line at a power level of minus 8 dbm, and the receive level is measured at minus 16 dbm. Further suppose that the MODEM applies the space frequency (2200 Hz) at minus 8 dbm, and that the receive level is again minus 16 dbm. Since the amount of loss is the same in both cases, the telephone circuit attenuates the signals by 8 dbm, or. has 8 dbm of attenuation. Figure J-1 illustrates the relationship between input and output FSK waveforms after ordinary attenuation has occurred.

Attenuation distortion is a type of power loss in which the frequencies under consideration are *not* affected equally. In a circuit or system, attenuation distortion refers to a departure from uniform amplification or attenuation over the frequency range required for transmission, or unequal amplification within the bandpass.

There are several possible causes of attenuation distortion. The most common cause in wired circuits is line reactance, which causes a change in line impedance (and a resulting mismatch of impedances) with a change in applied frequency. Other possible causes include nonlinear gain of amplifiers, problems in radio or carrier systems, and defective compensating circuits within the telephone network.

The most common method of expressing attenuation distortion is in terms of frequency response. If a signal generator is connected to the input terminals of a telephone circuit and a number of constant amplitude sample frequencies are applied, the output voltage at the remote terminals can be measured and graphed for each. If the sample frequencies encompass the circuit bandpass, the results are graphed similar to that shown in figure J-2.

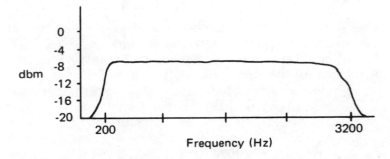

Fig. J-2   Theoretical frequency response graph

In figure J-2, the gain (or attenuation factor) of the circuit is approximately constant for all test frequencies between 200 and 3200 Hz. Attenuation distortion usually affects one end of the bandpass more than the other, and is described as "poor high-frequency response" or "poor low-frequency response." These are illustrated in figure J-3.

One method of testing for attenuation distortion (not an analysis, but an indicator) makes use of the MODEM. Attenuation distortion results in different circuit gain at different frequencies. The MODEM may be set up to transmit the mark frequency, and later the space frequency, in each case at the same transmit level. The level should be that which is normally applied to the circuit. The output levels of the circuit are measured at the remote terminal. If the mark frequency is attenuated more than the space

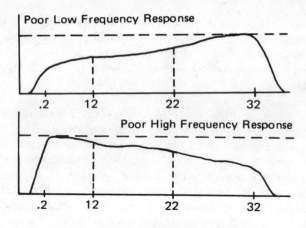

Fig. J-3 Effect of attenuation distortion

frequency, the circuit has poor low-frequency response. If the space frequency is attenuated more than the mark frequency, the circuit has poor high-frequency response. Attenuation distortion is usually tolerable until one of the frequencies is attenuated to a point exceeding circuit specifications. Even then, circuit operation may be acceptable depending on the amount of attenuation distortion, which of the frequencies is attenuated, the transmission rate, and the type of data application.

Figure J-4 illustrates the effect of attenuation distortion on an FSK waveform. Excessive attenuation of the space frequency is shown. If the circuit has poor low-frequency response instead, the amplitude of the mark frequency is the smaller of the two. The difference in amplitude is the amount of attenuation distortion between the two frequencies.

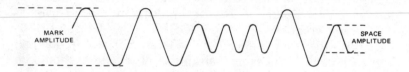

Fig. J-4 Effect of high frequency "attenuation distortion"

Attenuation frequency distortion refers to the effect which a circuit will produce in a complex waveform because of the limited bandpass and bandwidth of the circuit. Complex waveforms such as voice signals are composed of many fundamental frequencies and harmonics. When some of the fundamental frequencies or harmonics are eliminated because they are not within the circuit bandpass, the change in the complex waveform is described as attenuation frequency distortion.

The test instrument which measures attenuation frequency distortion is a spectrum analyzer. It is a receiver which automatically scans a portion of the frequency spectrum and displays a plot of amplitude versus frequency of the input signal on a cathode ray tube or chart. A comparison of spectrum analysis charts of the input and output signals leads to an accurate description of the attenuation frequency distortion occurring within the circuit.

Square waves are complex waveforms. Raw data signals are essentially square waves. In theory a square wave is composed of a fundamental sine wave frequency and an infinite number of *odd* harmonics (3, 5, 7, etc.). If a 1000 baud square wave is applied to a circuit which, because of its limited bandwidth, does not pass the odd harmonics (3000 Hz, 5000 Hz, etc.), the output from that circuit will be a nearly sinusoidal 1000 Hz waveform. Multiplying the baud rate by three (3) indicates the minimum acceptable circuit bandwidth for transmission of data and teletype signals. This means that a waveform three times the fundamental frequency (the third harmonic) must pass through the circuit if the waveform is to retain a semblance of its original square shape.

Since FSK waveforms are nearly sinusoidal, they are not affected by attenuation frequency distortion as drastically as square waveforms. Since FSK waveforms are not composed of higher odd harmonics the "multiply by three" rule does not apply and higher transmission rates are attainable. Attenuation frequency distortion is seldom a problem in FSK transmission.

NOISE

Electrical and electronic noise is a complex subject; not all technicians agree as to what constitutes noise in electrical circuits. In this description, noise is defined as *unwanted* and *unintelligible* signals. Some technicians insist that any signal, intelligible or otherwise, is noise if it is present in the circuit and should not be present.

Two types of noise are *random* noise and *impulse* noise. Random noise refers to the average power level of all noise frequencies present, and impulse noise refers to the higher amplitude noise peaks which exceed a stated value. Impulse noise is a part of the measured random noise.

Many factors contribute to noise in electrical circuits. Thermal noise is produced when heat causes molecular agitation in materials. Amplifiers, filters and other electrical circuits each introduce particular types of noise. Atmospheric disturbances which contribute to noise in electrical circuits may be natural (lightning, sunspots, etc.) or artificial (motor, generators, diathermy and X-ray machines, etc.).

The amount of noise in a telephone circuit is the product of many variables. It depends to some extent on the length and environment of the transmission medium, types of modulation methods, volume of message traffic, and even to some extent on the time of day, week, or year. The amount of noise usually increases during periods of peak telephone use, and noise measurements at a given instant are usually not valid for other times. Therefore, noise is customarily measured and plotted over a period of time, providing a graph of average and peak values of the random noise level in a particular circuit. The graphs showing peak noise periods are often helpful in determining the best time of day for data transmission.

Random noise in electrical circuits is often called white noise. White noise is continuous and is distributed uniformly across the frequency spectrum. But the random noise is seldom continuous or composed of equal parts of all frequencies. Random noise often includes dominant

Fig. J-5   Circuit for random noise measurement

noise frequencies which are outside the bandpass of the voice channel. These noise frequencies are measurable but do not affect transmission through the channel. In order to obtain *valid* random noise measurements, appropriate filters must be used which remove those noise frequencies outside of the channel bandpass. The filters are discussed in more detail in the next section.

Random noise levels are usually measured in RMS volts or dbm. The amount of noise is expressed as a ratio of signal amplitude to noise amplitude, and is called the signal-to-noise ratio (snr). A more exact term in our application is "signal-plus-noise to noise ratio", abbreviated s+n/n. As used in this text, the term snr, it means s+n/n.

The snr is obtained through a measurement at the receive termination. An appropriate (usually 600-ohm) resistor is substituted for the receive MODEM. A 1000-Hz test frequency is applied at the transmit termination and at the appropriate transmit level. The voltage measurement across the 600-ohm resistor at the receive termination is the signal-plus-noise level. The 1000-Hz test tone is then removed from the input terminals (but the line remains terminated in its correct impedance) and another measurement is made at the receive terminals. This measurement is the noise level. The ratio of s+n to n equals the snr. Figure J-5 is used as an example of measuring and calculating the snr.

Assume that the signal-plus-noise level in figure J-5 measures 0.245 volts RMS. When the 1000-Hz tone is turned off at the transmitter, the remaining noise measures 0.0245 volts RMS. The signal-to-noise ratio equals 0.245/0.0245 or 10:1. Since the impedances are alike, this can be expressed in decibels by using the following formula:

$$db = 20 \log_{10} \frac{E\text{-}1}{E\text{-}2}$$

$$= 20 \log_{10} \frac{0.245}{0.0245}$$

$$= 20 \log_{10} (10)$$

$$= (20)(1.0000)$$

$$= 20 \, db.$$

Therefore, a signal-to-noise ratio of 10:1 is the same as a snr of 20 db if the impedances are the same. The dbm conversion chart in section I also shows that the snr can be obtained by subtracting one reading from the other in dbm. In the example the s+n measurement was 0.245 volts RMS or -10 dbm. The noise measurement was 0.0245 volts RMS or -30 dbm. Subtracting the noise level from the signal-plus-noise provides (-10-(-30)) or a snr of 20 db.

A different method of expressing noise ratios is often used for telephone circuits. This expression is the dbrnC, where db is a ratio, rn indicates random noise, and C indicates that a particular filter (C message type) is used in the measurement. Noise in dbrnC is stated as a positive number above a -90 dbm reference level. (A different filter, called the FIA, uses -85 dbm as the reference). Figure J-6 shows the relationship between dbm measurements and dbrnC measurements.

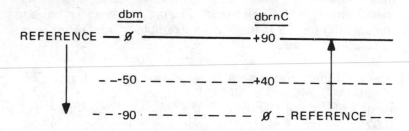

Fig. J-6   Equivalence of dbm and dbrnC measurements

In figure J-6, 0 dbm is the reference level and -90 dbm is a very small signal amplitude. This small amplitude corresponds to 0 dbrnC, which is the reference for noise measurements expressed in this manner. Conversion from dbm to dbrnC or the reverse is simple. The dbm value is subtracted from 90 to find the corresponding dbrnC value. For example, figure J-6 shows that -50 dbm corresponds to +40 dbrnC (90 - 50). Noise measurements in dbrnC are discussed in more detail in section L.

Providing that proper precautionary measures are taken concerning reference frequency, transmit level, filtering, and correct termination impedances, valid noise measurements can be obtained with standard test equipment. Special (and expensive) test equipment is required for a thorough analysis of the noise characteristics of a circuit, but a MODEM may sometimes be used to obtain an indication of excessive noise levels in a circuit. The MODEM is conditioned to transmit the mark frequency (which is close to the 1000-Hz test tone); the receive-level snr is measured with a meter as described earlier. While the readings obtained are not entirely accurate they may indicate when the noise level of a circuit is completely unacceptable. Figure J-7 depicts an FSK waveform which is combined with random noise.

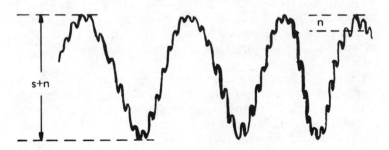

Fig. J-7   signal-plus-noise waveform

Impulse noise refers to the higher-amplitude peaks in a noise waveform. It is measured as the number of counts (times) that the noise exceeds a predetermined level (for example, 65 dbrn) in a fixed amount of time. Impulse noise may be caused by dialing circuits, relay contacts, motors, or any other device causing high-amplitude electric fields to be generated. Figure J-8 illustrates impulse-noise peaks in a random noise waveform.

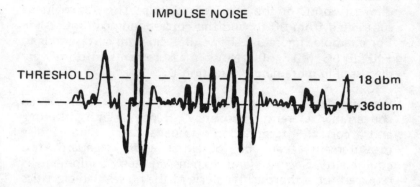

IMPULSE NOISE

THRESHOLD

18 dbm

36 dbm

Fig. J-8   Noise waveform showing impulse noise

Measurements are performed with a test set called an impulse-noise counter. The threshold is adjusted to the appropriate level and the appropriate filter is a part of the test set. Each time a noise pulse exceeds the threshold level, a count is registered on a meter. The number of counts per fixed amount of time (typically 15 or 30 minutes) is used as a criterion for determining the acceptability of the circuit. During periods of measurements, the FSK signal is not applied to the circuit because the measuring set can not distinguish between impulse noise and FSK waveforms.

Most EDP technicians do not have occasion to use an impulse-noise counter. If the circuit operation is not acceptable and impulse-noise seems to be the probable cause, the best approach is to contact the telephone company or Technical Service Department and arrange for accurate measurements. Generally, the impulse-noise count increases as random noise increases, and random noise measurements may indicate the need for more precise impulse-noise measurements.

CROSSTALK

Crosstalk is a type of interference which appears in a given channel but originates in a different channel. Crosstalk appears most often as background conversations and dialing pulses heard over normal telephone receivers. Crosstalk may be intelligible or unintelligible, depending on the amount which reaches the channel. The most significant effect of crosstalk on data transmission occurs when it is composed of high-amplitude, short-duration pulses which constitute impulse noise in the circuit.

There are several possible sources of crosstalk signals. These are voice, fascimile, teletype, dialing or ringing signals, or even different data signals. Crosstalk signals may be induced into a circuit in many ways and at any point in the transmission medium.

Crosstalk may occur when signals are transferred through multiconductor cables. Within the cables, wires are in close proximity to one another and currents in one pair of wires may generate magnetic fields which induce corresponding currents in nearby wires. This effect is called inductive coupling and is a common source of crosstalk. Capacitive coupling between wires may also account for signal transfer from one pair of wires to another.

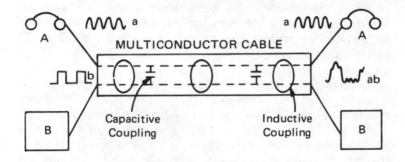

Fig. J-9   Crosstalk in a multiconductor cable

Carrier systems may also permit certain amounts of crosstalk. If channel-separation filters fail or are of poor quality, information from one channel may be present in other channels after demultiplexing. Since crosstalk has already occurred; it is practically impossible to eliminate the unwanted intelligence signal at that point. The same effect often occurs in microwave radio systems. The phrase which best describes this particular type of crosstalk is "adjacent-channel interference."

Sometimes telephone lines pass close to a radio station, or are long enough to act as receiving antennas, and radio signals are induced into the telephone circuits.

On the other hand, crosstalk may occur at the receiving-terminal location, rather than in transmission lines. When the crosstalk source is external to the telephone circuit, the telephone company cannot exercise control over it, even though the effect can be as devastating to data transmission as crosstalk in a multiconductor-cable or carrier system. In this case even an alternate route or alternate channel may not prove satisfactory.

One controllable factor which often contributes to crosstalk is overdriving a circuit by exceeding the transmit level specification. Increasing the transmit level to compensate for attenuation in the circuit is acceptable to a point, but the person who exceeds that point does not know that he is a source of crosstalk unless he is listening to adjacent channels. Most telephone companies specify a maximum input power level of 0 dbm for this reason, and individual telephone companies often specify a much lower (-8 to -13 dbm) transmit level.

If crosstalk is present in a particular communications channel, the best approach is switching to a different channel or route. If that is impossible, attempts should be made to have the telephone company monitor the circuit during peak periods of crosstalk. It is in the best position to identify the source and take corrective action. Technicians should also ensure that their transmit levels do not exceed specifications to avoid becoming a source of crosstalk.

ECHOES AND REFLECTIONS

Impedances should be matched to obtain maximum transfer of power. Also if the impedance is not constant throughout a long telephone line, some of the power may be reflected from the point of impedance mismatch back toward the source. In voice transmission the reflected power arrives at some later time and sounds like an echo. The effect is not harmful in voice transmission because humans recognize the echo for what it is and ignore it. Business machines simply respond to signals as they exist on the transmission line, and echoes may cause data errors.

Figure J-10 illustrates an echo resulting from direct connection of an open-wire line and a cable pair. Since the impedances of the two transmission lines are different, direct connection results in a mismatch of impedances.

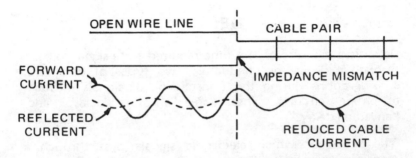

Fig. J-10   Effect of impedance mismatch

In figure J-10, the impedance mismatch causes reflections of the waveform. The reflected waveform algebraically adds to the original waveform and causes it to be distorted. In addition, the output voltage from the cable is reduced by the amount of the reflected voltage. Even if the distortion and reduction in amplitude are not enough to cause data transmission problems, the reduction in amplitude contributes to a poorer snr and the effect of random and impulse noise in the circuit becomes more pronounced.

The time delay between generation of the original waveform and the return of the reflected waveform depends on the length of the circuit and the particular point where impedances are mismatched. The delay may vary from a few milliseconds in a 200 mile circuit to 75 or so milliseconds in the New-York-to-London transatlantic cable. Echo delay-times in satellite communications may be as long as one-half second. Generally, the greater the time delay of an echo, the more likely it is to cause data transmission quality to deteriorate.

Within the telephone circuit, impedance-matching devices are used to reduce echoes and reflections. These are discussed in the next section. Echo suppressors, also discussed later, are often inserted in 4-wire trunk lines when the propagation times exceeds 40 or 50 milliseconds. The technician may do his part to reduce echoes and reflections by ensuring that the terminations are always connected to the correct impedances.

DELAY

Delay is a measure of the time required for a signal to pass through a device or conductor. Two types of delay are considerations during the transmission of signals through telephone circuits. These are "absolute delay" and "envelope delay."

The speed at which electronic signals pass through a transmission medium is called the velocity of propogation. Radio waves in free space travel at nearly the speed of light, and the velocity of propogation is 186 000 miles-per-second (300 000 000 meters-per-second). In all other transmission mediums, the velocity of propogation is slower because of the reactive qualities of the line.

Every transmission medium causes a phase shift of the waveform. This can be demonstrated by assuming a theoretically perfect transmission line (no power loss or reactance) of given length to which a constant frequency is applied. For example, a 1000-Hz signal is applied to a perfect transmission line which is 46.5 miles long. Figure J-11 illustrates the transmission line and input waveform.

One cycle of the input signal lasts 360 degrees. The period of the input signal is 1 msec. Therefore, each 90 degrees of the input signal represents an absolute time of 250 usec.

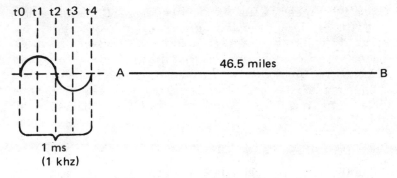

Fig. J-11   Theoretical transmission line

The amount of time required for the electrical signal to travel from point A to point B in figure J-11 is equal to the distance divided by the speed. Solving for time provides:

$$t = \frac{d}{s} = \frac{46.5}{186,000} = 250 \text{ microseconds}$$

Therefore, if one cycle of a 1000-Hz signal is applied, and the beginning of the cycle is designated as t_0, this part of the waveform appears at point B 250 microseconds after it is present at point A. The amount of delay is 250 microseconds and is a function of the length of the transmission line. A simultaneous display of the input and output waveforms appears as shown in figure J-12.

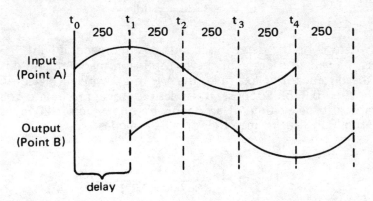

Fig.   J-12   1000-Hz waveforms

125

Since 90 degrees of the waveform equals 250 microseconds and the amount of delay equals 250 microseconds, the phase difference between input and output waveforms is 90 degrees. It should be obvious that the phase shift in degrees depends on line length *and* frequency. Doubling the input frequency to this transmission line does not change the delay time, but it results in a phase shift of 180 degrees at the 2000-Hz rate.

Above a certain reference frequency (nominal 4000 to 10,000 Hz), the velocity of propogation is relatively constant for all frequencies. A characteristic of different types of wired transmission mediums is that the average velocity through each depends upon the type, size, and shape of the conductors, the relationship to other conductors and earth, and the type of dielectric insulating-material used. The phrase which describes this characteristic is "velocity factor" (VF). The VF of a transmission line is a ratio of the average velocity of propogation through that line to the speed of light.

The velocity factory is useful in approximating the absolute delay of a given transmission line. Absolute delay is a measure of the time between transmission and reception of a single frequency. The absolute delay between any two points can be calculated using the formula:

$$D_t = \frac{1}{(s)\ (VF)}\ (d)$$

where D_t is the delay in seconds, s is the speed of light, VF is the velocity factor of the transmission medium, and d is the distance. For example, the VF of a 2-wire air dielectric line is 0.975. Suppose it is desired to approximate the absolute delay time of an open-wire line which is 20-miles long. Substituting into the formula provides:

$$D_t = \frac{1}{186,000 \times 0.975}\ (20)$$

$$= 110 \text{ microseconds}$$

TYPE OF LINE		VF	DELAY ns/foot	us/mile	ns/meter	us/km
2 WIRE OPEN	(AIR)	0.975	1.04	5.50	3.42	3.42
COAXIAL	(AIR)	0.85	1.20	6.31	3.92	3.92
2 WIRE	(SOLID)	0.68	1.49	7,89	4.90	4.90
COAXIAL	(SOLID)	0.66	1.54	8.13	5.05	5.05

Table   J-1   Examples of absolute delay

The chart in table J-1 lists the VF and delay times of some typical wired transmission lines. The type of dielectric material is shown in parentheses for each example.

Absolute delay is primarily a function of the length of the transmission medium. The difference in *velocities* through different transmission mediums does not cause transmission problems because the signal elements are in reference to each other, rather than to the time of their origination. For these reasons absolute delay is seldom stated for telephone circuits, and measures of absolute delay are of little significance.

On the other hand, differences in velocity *between frequencies* can cause data transmission problems. The velocity of propogation of a single frequency is called the "phase velocity" of that frequency. Differences in phase velocity increase at lower frequencies, particularly below 4000 Hz. One of the factors which contributes to a difference in phase velocity is the inductive reactance of that line. A purely inductive circuit will shift the phase of a signal by 90 degrees, and an RL circuit will cause less than 90 degrees of phase shift.

A given transmission line has a fixed amount of inductance as one of its properties. As the frequency of the signal applied to the line increases, inductive reactance increases. Since inductive reactance is opposition to current flow, the higher frequency signals encounter greater opposition to their travel along the line. This seems to mean that higher frequencies travel along the line more slowly than low frequencies.

However, as the frequency of the signal applied to the line

is increased, current tends to flow nearer the surface of the wire, away from the physical center. This phenomenon is called "skin effect" and effectively reduces the inductive reactance of the line, causing an increase in the phase velocity of higher-frequency signals.

Capacitance also affects the phase velocity in a transmission medium. Electrical signals in free space travel at the speed of light. In open-wire lines, the dielectric material is air (dielectric constant = 1), and the phase velocity is greater than for solid dielectric lines (dielectric constant >1). Ideally the dielectric constant (which in part determines the capacitance) is fixed for a particular material. In practice, the dielectric constant of a material changes with frequency. The change may be positive or negative (or both) and is nonlinear. The general trend over a range of frequencies is usually a reduction in the dielectric constant, giving rise to higher phase velocities for higher frequency signals.

A medium in which the phase velocity of a wave is related to frequency is called a dispersive medium. A prism is a dispersive medium. When a prism is used to separate white light into its component colors, the higher frequencies (violet) are refracted or bent more than the lower frequencies (red), as shown in figure J-13. This is the same as saying that higher frequencies travel slower through the medium (the prism) than lower frequencies. This became known as "normal" dispersion since curves were first compiled for such cases.

In a medium where the opposite is true (high frequencies have a greater velocity than low frequencies), the characteristic is described as "anomalous" dispersion. A given transmission line may exhibit no dispersion, normal dispersion, anomalous dispersion, or all three depending on the range of the applied frequencies. Figure J-14 illustrates the dispersive characteristic for a typical transmission medium.

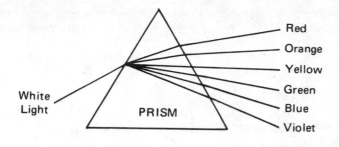

Fig. J-13   A dispersive medium

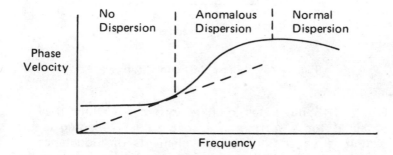

Fig. J-14   Typical phase velocity versus frequency curve

Telephone communications circuits generally exhibit either no dispersion or anomalous dispersion through the range of applied frequencies. In a standard open-wire line, the phase velocity is about 140 000 miles-per-second (mps) at 250 Hz, increasing to nearly 182 000 mps at 3000 Hz. By comparison, phase velocity varies from about 25 000 mps to 75 000 mps for the same frequencies if the transmission medium is one pair of wires in a multiconductor cable. It is noteworthy that the frequencies used in carrier terminal equipment (above 4 000 Hz) travel at nearly the same velocity in open-wire lines or cable pairs.

The velocity of a composite waveform as it moves along the transmission line is called the "group velocity" or "envelope velocity." Some of the frequencies in the envelope exceed the group velocity, and others pass through the circuit more slowly. The envelope (group) may contain any of the frequencies within the bandpass being considered.

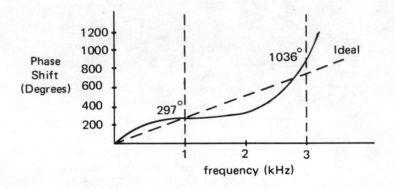

Fig. J-15   Phase shift curve (typical)

Figure J-15 illustrates a phase shift curve which may be obtained for a section of loaded cable. (Loading is the technique of adding lumped elements of inductance or capacitance at uniformly spaced intervals to improve the line characteristics.) The ideal phase shift at 3000 Hz is exactly three times the phase shift at 1000 Hz.

Delay distortion is a measure of the difference in arrival times of two different frequencies within the envelope. In the above example, the difference in arrival times can be computed by determing the difference in phase of the two signals (in degrees) and multiplying by the period of the frequency which is used as a reference. For example, if the period of the 3000-Hz signal (333 μsec.) is used as a reference, the delay distortion equals:

$$\frac{1036-(3 \times 297)}{360} \ (0.000,333) \ = \ 134\mu sec.$$

Conversely, if the period of the 1000 Hz signal (1 msec.) is used as the reference, the delay distortion is equal to:

$$\frac{(1036/3)-297}{360} \ (0.001) \ = \ 134\mu sec.$$

A 1000 Hz. signal is delayed 134 µsec. relative to the 3000 Hz signal. Statements of delay distortion are made with respect to another frequency and are valid *only* for these two.

It is difficult to transmit a single frequency through a circuit and measure its phase delay, because an accurate phase reference cannot be established unless both ends of the circuit are available at the same location. For this reason, measurements of envelope delay are more common. Envelope delay (ED) is measured by transmitting a narrow band amplitude modulated waveform through the circuit and comparing it to a generated reference (AM) at the receiver. The bandwidth of the AM waveform is very small (typically 50 Hz to 166 Hz) compared to the channel bandwidth. This method does not yield the true delay distortion obtained from the phase-shift curve, but has the advantage that it can be measured and corrected.

Envelope delay is a derivative of phase shift with respect to frequency, and represents the slope of the curve at that frequency. A frequency which undergoes the minimum absolute delay (typically 2000 Hz) is selected as the reference. The delay at this frequency is considered as 0, and other frequencies in the band have more or less (positive or negative) delay in respect to the reference. When the envelope delay at various frequencies is plotted in respect to his reference, a graph is produced similar to the one shown in figure J-16.

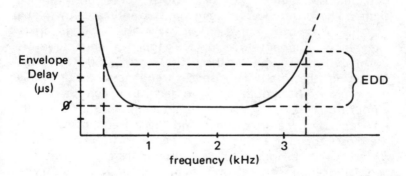

Fig. J-16   Envelope delay curve

From figure J-16, a specification of envelope delay distortion is the maximum measurable difference (worst case condition) in envelope delay in the band of frequencies of interest. The envelope delay characteristic of a particular circuit is the sum of the individual envelope delays of the circuit facilities (wired lines, carrier equipment, terminal equipment, etc.). Reflected waveforms also affect the envelope delay characteristic, and accurate determination of the envelope delay of a circuit is obtained only through the use of measurement sets.

Delay distortion can cause data transmission difficulties. It is possible in FSK transmission that one of the transmitted frequencies travels at a higher velocity than the other, causing overlapping of the data symbols during transition from the lower to the higher frequency, and gaps or voids in the waveform when changing from the higher to the lower frequency or the reverse. This intersymbol interference may cause data errors or marginal performance, and when combined with other marginal circuit parameters it may render the channel unacceptable for data transmission.

Envelope delay measuring sets contain a transmitter and a receiver. The transmitter generates a reference AM waveform and a testing AM waveform. The reference carrier frequency (R) is fixed and the testing carrier frequency (S) is variable through the band. The testing waveform is transmitted through the circuit, and the phase of the detected AM signal is compared to the detected reference signal. The difference between the two indicates the slope of the phase-shift curve at or near the testing carrier frequency. The envelope delay (slope of the curve) is normally minimum in the 1500- to 2000-Hz range. Centering the mark and space frequencies around this minimum point should result in each undergoing a similar amount of delay. Also, reducing the bandwidth of the FSK envelope by generating mark and space frequencies which are closer together reduces the delay distortion because the difference in propagation velocities is lessened. (But this generally requires more sophisticated detection circuitry in the receive MODEM.)

Two basic envelope delay test methods are illustrated in

figure J-17. When the end-to-end method is used, a carrier frequency is generated and modulated at the transmitter. The AM waveform is transmitted through the circuit where the USB, LSB, and carrier each undergo slightly different amounts of phase shift. At the receiver the waveform is demodulated and compared to a locally generated reference of constant phase.

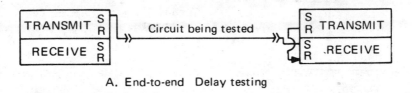

A. End-to-end Delay testing

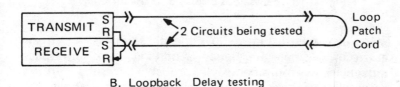

B. Loopback Delay testing

Fig. J-17   Envelope delay measurement methods

When the loopback testing method is used, the testing AM signal (S) is transmitted through one telephone circuit and using jumpers or patch cords is returned to the same location through a different circuit. Dividing the envelope delay by 2 approximates the envelope delay of each circuit. This test method is not wholly accurate because the delay characteristics of the circuits may differ.

A method of approximating the phase delay of a circuit with an oscilloscope displays the Lissajous pattern obtained by comparing the phase of the transmitted signal to that of the received signal. Both ends of the circuit under test must be available at the same location, or the loopback method may be used. Figure J-18 illustrates the basic test configuration. Figure J-19 illustrates the Lissajous patterns for different amounts of phase shifts.

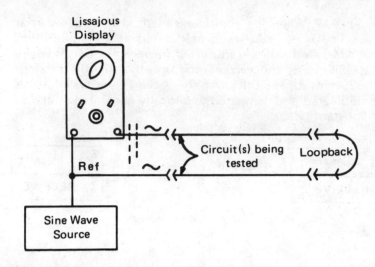

Fig. J-18   Lissajous display of phase differences

These Lissajous displays show the phase difference in the return of a single frequency. Applying mark and space frequencies simultaneously probably results in a meaningless display. If the circuit is relatively short, the Lissajous display accurately indicates phase shift. If the circuit is of sufficient length that the phase shift exceeds $180°$, it may be difficult to determine from the observed pattern since, for example, the pattern at $45°$ and $315°$ of phase shift is identical.

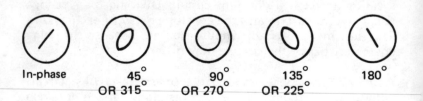

Fig.   J-19   Lissajous patterns

A third method of determining the relative time delay between two signals makes use of an oscilloscope to display the so-called eye pattern. A repetitive sequence of ONES and ZEROES is converted to FSK, transmitted through the circuit, and displayed on an oscilloscope. Adjustment of the sweep time will produce a display similar to that shown in figure J-20. Thickness of the line (vertical amplitude) at point A indicates the amount of attenuation distortion, and width (horizontal amplitude) of the line at point B indicates the relative time delay between the mark and space frequencies.

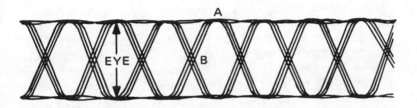

Fig. J-20   Eye pattern

Observation of the eye pattern does indicate the presence of delay distortion, but it is difficult to arrive at an accurate measure of the distortion from the pattern. Display of the eye pattern is more commonly used when the circuit delay is being adjusted. At this time the exact amount of delay distortion is not important. Adjustment of the delay compensating circuitry produces changes in the eye pattern which are readily observable and which indicate the result of the particular adjustment.

OTHER TRANSMISSION PROBLEMS

Jitter describes an instability of the leading and trailing edges of the received data waveform. Jitter is shown in figure J-21. It typically occurs at rates of 180 Hz and below and is usually caused by power-supply ripple in the transmission equipment.

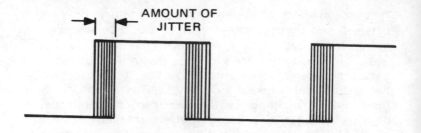

Fig. J-21 Jitter of a data waveform

Frequency error may occur in the received FSK signals because of differences between the carrier frequencies in the carrier terminal equipment. If the reinserted carrier frequency is not exactly the same as the original carrier frequency, the FSK frequencies will differ by a like amount. For example, if the FSK frequency is 1200 Hz and the difference between the multiplexer and demultiplexer carrier frequencies is 5 Hz, the received FSK signal will be either 1195 Hz or 1205 Hz, depending on the particular multiplexing technique. The usual frequency-error goal in long distance dedicated circuits is ±10 Hz.

Amplitude nonlinearity may occur in circuits. Some common causes include saturation, cutoff and crossover distortion in amplifiers, harmonic distortion, and waveform compression. Amplitude distortion is normally low enough that transmission rates of 1200 baud and below are unaffected.

Hits are momentary line disturbances which may result in mutilation of the data characters. *Dropouts* are separate, distinct and discrete short term variations in signal level which may result in transmission errors. Little is known of the causes of hits and dropouts. No attempt is made to predict or control them. If the number of hits or dropouts is excessive, the circuits must be treated individually, because circuit unacceptability due to hits and dropouts is a rare occurrence.

Insertion loss is a reduction in amplitude which results when circuits are connected together. In telephone circuits the line impedance is normally within 40 percent of its rated 600-ohm value which indicates that the amount of insertion loss is frequency dependent. Typical amplitude loss across the interface is in the range of 10 to 16 dbm.

SUMMARY

Numerous transmission problems degrade the quality of telephone-circuit transmissions. Attenuation relative to noise level, attenuation distortion, and attenuation frequency distortion alter signal waveforms between the input and output of a circuit. Noise, crosstalk, echoes, reflections, and delays interfere with the desired signal during transmission, causing errors to be introduced into data signals. These degrading influences must be recognized and described by the online technician in his repair tasks and in his communication with telephone-company technicians.

QUESTIONS

Answers to the following questions are listed in Appendix III.

1. What is the word or phrase which describes equal power loss at all frequencies under consideration?

2. "Poor high frequency response" is a form of _____ _____ .

3. How may the data set be used to indicate frequency response of a telephone circuit?

4. What characteristics of a circuit cause attenuation frequency distortion?

5. What is noise in an electrical circuit?

6. What are the two categories or types of noise measured in telephone circuits?

7. List some factors which contribute to noise in electrical circuits.

8. What circuit element is necessary during noise measurements to ensure that valid readings are obtained?

9. What is the reference for noise readings in dbrn?

10. A snr of 68 dbrn indicates that noise level in the circuit should not exceed _____ dbm.

11. How are measures of impulse noise expressed?

12. List some possible causes of impulse noise.

13. Where do crosstalk signals usually originate?

14. Two types of coupling which may account for crosstalk are _____ and _____ _____ .

15. Describe three approaches to circuit problems involving excessive crosstalk?

16. What is the main cause of echoes and reflections in transmission lines?

17. What affects the time delay between transmission of a signal and return of the echo?

18. Which factor about transmission lines causes absolute delay?

19. What is delay distortion?

20. Which quality of a transmission medium causes delay distortion?

21. Why is it more common practice in telephone circuits to measure envelope-delay distortion rather than absolute delay distortion?

22. What part of the voice channel bandwidth normally encounters the minimum absolute delay?

23. What two oscilloscope displays indicate absolute delay or delay distortion?

24. Instability of the leading and trailing edges of a data waveform is described as _____ .

25. If the multiplex and demultiplex carrier frequencies differ by a 5 Hz the frequency error between transmitted and received signals is __Hz.

26. Momentary short-term variations in signal level or phase are described as _____ or _____ .

27. A normal reduction in amplitude when circuits are c o n n e c t e d t o g e t h e r i s c a l l e d
_____ _____ .

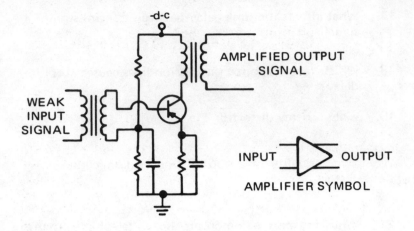

Fig. K-1   Amplifier circuit and symbol

Figure K-2 shows how amplifiers are connected in a transmission line to compensate for line losses. The power-level diagram below illustrates the signal power level at various points along the transmission line.

In figure K-2, each section of the transmission line has a fixed amount of attenuation. The amplifiers are inserted at appropriate points to raise the signal power level to the desired point. If there were no amplifiers in the circuit, the receive level at the central office would be –56 dbm, the sum of all the line losses.

Figure K-3 shows the power-level diagram in respect to random noise level at points along the transmission line.

The amplifiers respond to noise as well as signal. In this example the noise level shown varies around –50 dbm (40 dbrn).

K Corrective Elements in Telephone Circuits

Communicating through telephone circuits is not a simple operation. Many of the transmission parameters and considerations which affect communication have already been described. Considering just the factors which affect signal transfer through wired lines, it is obvious that signal quality deteriorates rapidly with increasing distance. Communications between New York and Chicago would be practically impossible if the transmission line were simply a pair of wires.

This section presents brief descriptions of some of the elements and techniques used by telephone companies to correct and control transmission parameters and enhance long-distance communications. Detailed theory is avoided, and the discussions tend more toward overview and concept.

AMPLIFIERS

Amplifiers are used in telephone circuits to overcome attenuation losses and to control snr. Amplifier circuits are usually transistorized, plug-in modules with adjustable gain controls; they are used in conjunction with amplitude equalizer circuits. Most telephone circuits have one or more amplifiers in the transmission path, particularly in interoffice or toll trunks.

A basic amplifier circuit is illustrated in figure K-1. Telephone line amplifiers typically are adjustable to provide a maximum gain of 30 db and a maximum output-power level in the area of +10 dbm, but they are seldom operated at their maximum because of possible amplitude distortion.

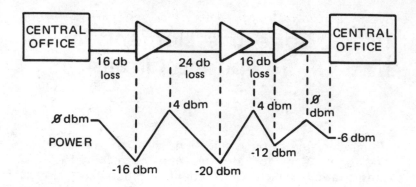

Fig. K-2 Amplifier installation in transmission lines

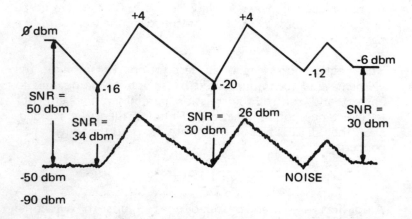

Fig. K-3 Signal power level versus noise power level diagram

Figure K-3 illustrates that the amplifiers raise both noise and signal-power levels. The snr at any point is equal to the difference between signal-power level and noise-power level. As the signal passes along the transmission medium, the snr changes and at the receive terminals is equal to the worst-case condition in the transmission medium. However, if amplifiers were not used in the circuit, the signal-power level would be smaller than the noise level at the remote end of the circuit and the signal could not be distinguished from the noise.

In telephone circuits, amplifiers are often combined with

hybrid transformers into units called repeaters. A simple repeater for use in 4-wire is illustrated in figure K-4.

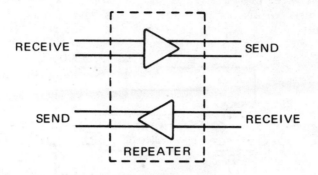

Fig. K-4   A 4-wire repeater

A repeater configuration for 2-wire lines is shown with associated hybrid and balancing circuits in figure K-5.

Signals from either direction pass through the circuit and are amplified by their respective amplifier. The hybrid circuits reduce the generation of sideband frequencies and the balance circuits maintain electrical balance of the signals with respect to ground.

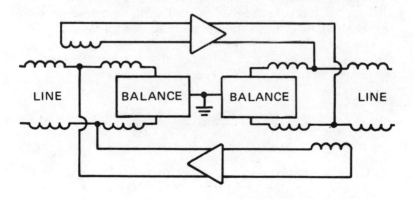

Fig.   K-5   A 2-wire repeater

The last type of repeater discussed here has a special application. It is called a terminal repeater. Most subscriber terminations are 2-wire circuits, while most toll and trunk lines are 4-wire circuits. The terminal repeater diagramed in figure K-6 functions as a 2-to-4-wire converter or a 4-to-2-wire converter and is used in the connections between subscriber (2-wire) circuits and trunk (4-wire) circuits.

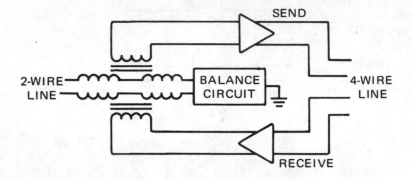

Fig. K-6   Terminal repeater

IMPEDANCE MATCHING DEVICES

Impedance matching devices are needed to maximize transfer of power and to minimize echoes and reflections. Three methods of impedance matching in common use employ matching transformers, pads, and amplifiers.

Currents, voltages and impedances of transformer windings are related to the turns ratio according to the formula:

$$\frac{Np}{Ns} = \frac{Ep}{Es} = \frac{Is}{Ip} = \sqrt{\frac{Zp}{Zs}}$$

Np/Ns is the ratio of the number of turns in the primary winding to the number of turns in the secondary winding of the transformer and E, I, and Z are the respective primary and secondary voltages, currents, and impedances.

The formula shows that changing the primary-to-secondary turns ratio also changes the impedance ratio. Therefore, transformers can be selected which match practically any impedance to any other impedance. But transformers are not used for impedance matching in all cases because they have power loss, and to some extent they respond better to one frequency than others.

Three other applications of transformers are balancing, isolation, and bridging. The use of transformers for converting from balanced to unbalanced lines or the reverse is illustrated in figure K-7. The transformer also matches circuit impedances to each other.

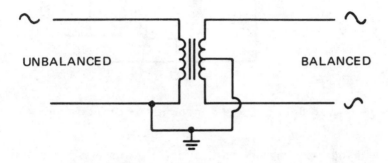

UNBALANCED   BALANCED

Fig. K-7   Transformer balanced to unbalanced connections

Either side of the transformer can be considered as the input and the other side as the output. Hence the circuit can be used to convert from balanced to unbalanced circuits or the reverse. Balanced lines are most frequently used for dedicated and trunk circuits because of their relative immunity to noise. Noise signals are induced on both wires at the same level and polarity, and they therefore cancel each other at the balanced termination.

Isolation transformers are used to prevent d.c. connection between two points while passing a.c. signals between the points. As illustrated in figure K-8, most MODEMS have an isolation and impedance-matching transformer in their output circuits. A prime function of the transformer is prevention of current flow between the business machine ground and the central office ground. While each earth ground is a reference point for the associated signals and circuits, the two grounds may not be at the same potential.

Connecting the grounds through a low resistance wire may result in heavy currents at power line frequencies and damage to the equipment. Care should be exercised during measurement to ensure that the test equipment does *not* place an earth ground on either of the subscriber lines.

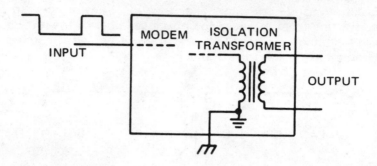

Fig. K-8   Use of transformers for circuit isolation

Bridging transformers have a single primary winding and multiple secondary windings. These are used when the same intelligence signal is supplied to many terminals at the same time. Each output of the bridging transformer is called a port. A basic bridging transformer circuit is shown in figure K-9.

The circuit in figure K-9 is called a 4-port bridge. Ports 1, 2, and 3 are connected to different terminal devices. Note that port 4 is terminated with a 600-ohm resistor. Each port of the bridge *MUST* be terminated in the correct impedance to ensure that the primary winding presents the correct impedance to the telephone circuit. An unused and unterminated port causes an impedance mismatch at the primary winding.

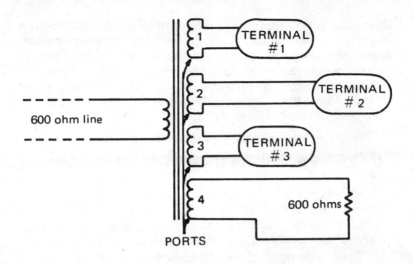

Fig. K-9   Bridging transformer connections

"Pads" are networks of selected resistors connected in a configuration which matches impedances and inserts known attenuation loss in the circuit. Pads are usually supplied and installed by the telephone company and calculation of pad values is not described in this text. Pads are typically rated according to the amount of power loss they cause in a circuit. For example, an "8 db pad" may be inserted in each receive line to reduce signal amplitude at the subscriber receiving location. Some common pad circuits are illustrated in figure K-10.

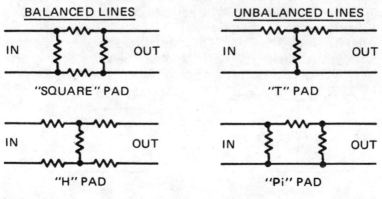

Fig. K-10   Common pad circuits

147

Amplifier and repeater circuits may also function as impedance matching devices. The common-emitter transistor amplifier normally used in the circuit has an input impedance in the range of 500 to 1500 ohms and an output impedance in the range of 20 000 to 500 000 ohms. Input and output transformers match the impedance of the amplifier circuit to the respective segments of the telephone line.

FILTERS

Previous discussions have emphasized the importance of filters in the carrier terminal equipment multiplexing and demultiplexing processes, in noise measurements, and for shaping the bandwidth, bandpass, and frequency response of the circuits. The following are basic circuit configurations and frequency-response characteristics of some common filters.

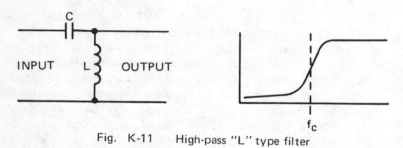

Fig. K-11   High-pass "L" type filter

The high-pass filter circuit shown in figure K-11 passes all frequencies from input to output which are above the reference cutoff frequency (f_c). Lower frequencies are attenuated by the filter. The cutoff frequency is a function of the combined values of L and C. The slope of the curve at f_c is a function of ratio of capacitance to inductance.

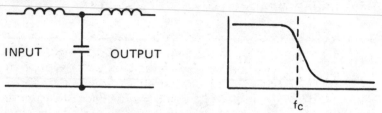

Fig. K-12   Low-pass "T" type filter

Low-pass filters attenuate higher frequencies while passing lower frequencies. Note that undesired frequencies are not completely eliminated by filters. They are attenuated by an amount which depends on the values of L and C, resistance of the coil, impedance and impedance matching in the circuit,and the particular frequency which is applied. Figure K-12 shows a "T"-type low-pass filter.

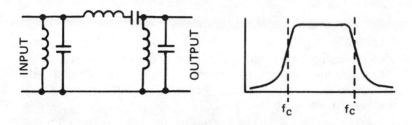

Fig. K-13   Complex bandpass filter

Connecting different values of L and C in series and parallel configurations produces a complex filter. A bandpass filter is a complex filter. The bandpass filter has two cutoff frequencies. All frequencies between these two pass through the circuit with little attenuation, while frequencies outside the desired bandpass are greatly attenuated. This type of filter has many applications in telephone circuits, particularly in the multiplexing and demultiplexing equipment. Figure K-13 shows a complex bandpass filter.

The band-reject filter shown in figure K-14 also has two cutoff frequencies. In the case of the band-reject filter, signals between the two cutoff frequencies are attenuated and all others are passed by the circuit. Band reject filters are often used to separate dialing and ringing supervisory tones from other signals in telephone circuits.

Two special filters mentioned earlier are the "F1A" filter and the "C message" filter. Numerous experiments with telephone receivers and the interference effects of noise on speech signals have produced desirable frequency-response curves for voice circuits. Tailoring the frequency response by using appropriate filters is called "weighting" the circuit.

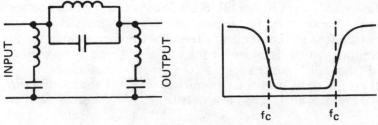

Fig. K-14   Complex band-reject filter

F1A weighting is based on the frequency response of the F1A receiver used in the Bell 302 telephone set. Measurements of noise based on F1A weighting are described in "dbrn adjusted" or *dba* and based on a -85 dbm reference level.

The newer Bell 500 telephone set has a different frequency response and requires a different weighting filter for measurements. The filter designed for measurements in this system is called a C message filter. Statements of noise levels with C message weighting are in dbrnC and are based on a −90 dbm reference level. C message weighting is more commonly used. Current noise-measurement sets usually have provision for switching C message, 3 kHz flat, or 15 kHz flat filters into the circuit being tested. Figure K-15 illustrates the frequency response differences between 3 kHz flat, C message, and F1A weighting curves.

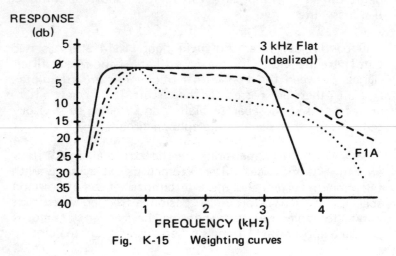

Fig. K-15   Weighting curves

EQUALIZERS

Two types of equalizers are used in telephone circuits. These are amplitude equalizers and delay equalizers.

A wired transmission line, because of its inherent series inductance and shunt capacitance, is essentially a low-pass filter. A normal condition in lengthy wired circuits is that higher frequencies suffer greater attenuation than lower frequencies. Amplitude equalizers are usually inserted in the lines with amplifiers or repeaters which compensate for this effect. Figure K-16 shows the basic amplitude equalizer circuit. The parallel L-C circuit is tuned to higher frequencies within the desired circuit bandpass. As a result lower-frequency signals are attenuated a greater amount than higher-frequency signals. The adjustable resistor varies the effect which the L-C circuit will have, and therefore it controls the difference in attenuation between high- and low-frequency signals.

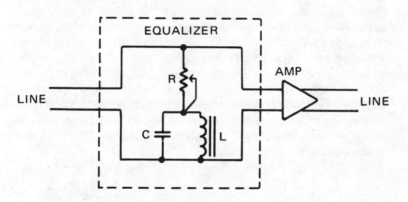

Fig. K-16   Basic amplitude equalizer circuit

Figure K-17 illustrates the desired effect of the equalizer-amplifier circuit shown in figure K-16. The original band of frequencies input to the telephone circuit are equal in amplitude. After passing through a section of the telephone line, the band of frequencies has experienced ordinary attenuation and attenuation distortion (poor high frequency response) as shown in the left-hand chart in figure K-17.

151

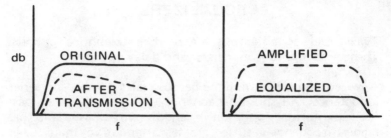

Fig. K-17   Function of equalizer-amplifier circuits

The right-hand chart in figure K-17 shows how the amplitude equalizer reduces the amplitude of lower frequencies causing the curve to be flat across the top. At this point the signals appear to have been affected by only ordinary attenuation. The amplifier then compensates for ordinary attentuation by increasing the power level of signals within the band to that level required for retransmission.

Delay equalizers are similar in that the effect is frequency dependent, but a delay equalizer controls phase shift rather than amplitude. Many delay equalizer circuit configurations are used according to circuit requirements. Delay equalizing circuits are generally modular plug-in boards, and equalization is accomplished by substituting equalizer circuits. Repeating delay measurements indicate the effect of delay equalizer substitution or the effect can be noted by observing an "eye" pattern. Figure K-18 illustrates delay-equalizer response.

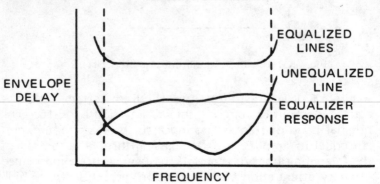

Fig. K-18   Delay-equalizer response

ECHO SUPPRESSORS

Many telephone companies which provide 2-wire subscriber service use 2-to-4-wire converters and transfer the signals through toil and interoffice trunks on 4-wire lines. At the opposite end of the circuit, another terminal repeater reconverts 2-wire service at that subscriber location. Slight impedance mismatches at the terminal repeaters may cause undesirable echoes in the reverse direction along the 4-wire line as illustrated in figure K-19.

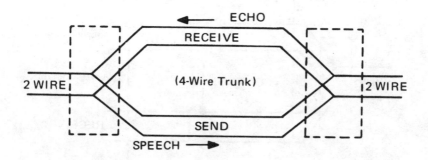

Fig. K-19   Echo effect in 2-to-4-wire converters

The echo is tolerable for voice and data communications in short-distance circuits. But in long-distance circuits, such as the New York to London transatlantic cable, the echo is delayed sufficiently to degrade communications. Echo suppressors are often inserted at both ends of such long distance circuits as shown in figure K-20.

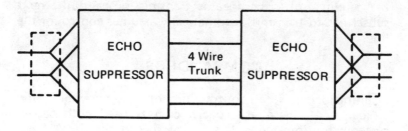

Fig. K-20   Echo-suppressor location in toll and carrier systems

An echo suppressor is composed of two amplifiers bridged across the send and receive lines as shown in figure K-21. When signals are applied to the send amplifiers, they produce a control voltage which disables the receive amplifier. This causes approximately 45 db of attenuation to be inserted in the receive line within 10 to 15 milliseconds after the signal is applied.

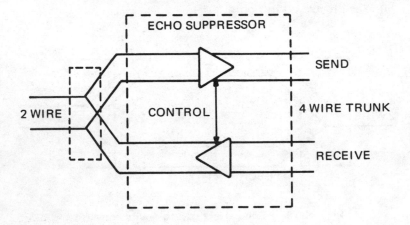

Fig. K-21   Echo-suppressor basic functions

During the period of time when the echo suppressor is enabled (blocking the receive path), signals are transferred in one direction only. It is essentially a half-duplex circuit depending upon which end of the circuit transmits first. The echo suppressor is automatically disabled shortly after the sending subscriber ceases transmission, and the next subscriber to transmit automatically assumes control of the line.

COMPANDERS

"Compander" is a contraction of "compressor" and "expander." These are special circuits used with carrier systems for improving the snr of speech signals. A basic compandered circuit is illustrated in figure K-22.

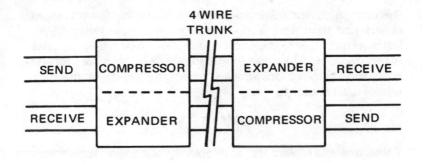

Fig. K-22   Basic circuit using companders

Voice signals occupy the amplitude range from approximately 0 dbm to -50 dbm. The compressor decreases the 50-db amplitude range to the approximately 18-db maximum variations for transmission. After transmission, the expander circuit recreates the original amplitude range and the voice signal sounds approximately normal. The basic advantage concerning noise is illustrated in the power level diagrams in figure K-23.

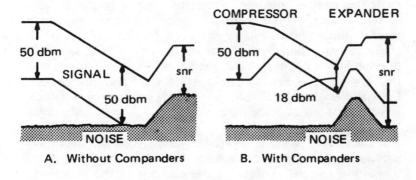

Fig. K-23   Effect of companders in a communications circuit

Figure K-23 illustrates how companders reduce the interference effect of random noise. Impulse noise effect is also reduced because the companders have slow response times, in the order of 4 to 8 changes-per-second maximum (approximating the syllable rates of speech). High amplitude, short duration noise peaks are attenuated for this reason. Since companders cannot distinguish the rapid changes of data signals in amplitude modulated waveforms from impulse noise, they should not be used when the data is in AM form. However, companders may provide impulse and random noise advantages when the levels of the data signals are constant.

SUMMARY

There are many factors in telephone and communications circuits which can degrade the quality of intelligence signals. These factors vary with line length, location type, and application. This section has presented a brief insight into some corrective circuits and techniques which compensate for deficiencies of the transmission lines.

Amplifiers combined with hybrid circuits form repeaters which compensate for attenuation losses. The terminal repeater also functions as a 2-to-4-wire converter. Amplitude equalizers compensate for the normal frequency response characteristic of the lines and delay equalizers for the normal delay-distortion characteristic. Impedance matching devices include transformers, pads, and amplifiers which reduce echoes, reduce power loss, and may have special applications. Filters are used for testing the noise characteristic, shaping the frequency response, and selecting or combining channels. Echo suppressors may be installed in lengthy circuits to reduce echoes and distortion. Companders are two section variable-gain devices which improve the snr of voice signals.

A subscriber seldom exercises any control over the location, quantity, or adjustment of corrective elements in telephone circuits. These are the domain of the telephone company. He normally leases the services of the telephone company in accordance with their specifications (as discussed in the next section), and the company installs, tests, and adjusts, the necessary corrective elements to provide the quality of service which the subscriber requires.

QUESTIONS

Answers to the following questions are listed in Appendix III.

1. List two functions of amplifiers as used in telephone circuits.

2. When calls are placed from 2-wire subscriber terminations through 4-wire trunks, the signals must pass through a _____ repeater.

3. Repeaters are amplifiers combined with _____ and _____ circuits.

4. Why are transformers not used in all cases for impedance matching?

5. List three applications of transformers other than impedance matching.

6. Why is it necessary that each port of a bridge be terminated in the correct impedance?

7. List four types of pad circuit configurations.

8. The high-pass filter attenuates _____ frequencies.

9. Which type of filter is used for most applications in telephone circuits?

10. What is "weighting" of a circuit?

11. Why are amplitude equalizers used in telephone circuits?

12. What is the function of a delay equalizer?

13. Echo suppressors are inserted in 4-wire trunks because of impedance mismatches at the _____ _____ _____ .

14. During periods of time when the echo suppressors are operational the 4-wire trunk circuit operates in the _____ _____ mode.

15. What is the basic function of companders in telephone circuits?

16. Why is compander removal sometimes necessary for data operation?

L Interpreting Circuit Specifications

Most telephone companies provide standard voice channels for use in the public switched network. These channels are not suitable for many applications. Most data subscribers have telephone channels conditioned (adjusted) to meet their requirements.

When installing and testing a new system or fault-finding in one which was previously operational, a technician must know the specifications of the particular circuit in order to evaluate channel quality. The circuit specifications are available from the telephone company which provides the service. The types and quality of telephone channels varies with location, application, and telephone company. There is no standard set of specifications which applies in all cases. Even individual telephone companies may change the specifications and tariffs of their channel offerings from time to time, which reinforces the idea that valid circuit evaluation may be made only after obtaining current specifications of the particular channel.

SELECTING A SERVICE

Dedicated line subscribers coordinate with the telephone company before the line is installed and conditioned. They select a basic channel and the channel-conditioning from a number of standards available. In special cases such as a narrow-band or broad-band channel requirement, the circuit parameters and tariffs are the result of negotiations between the telephone company and subscribers.

When the agreement is completed, the telephone company installs the subscriber terminations and routes the line through existing interoffice and toll systems. They install necessary corrective elements and condition the channel in accordance with the previous agreement. They usually supply the subscriber with a specification sheet of channel parameters at this time. The uninformed customer may not be aware of the value of this information to maintenance personnel, believing that one telephone line is the same as any other. If the installation has existed for some time, he may not even be aware that he possesses the information. In such cases the technician must take steps to ensure that he has valid, current information regarding the channel parameters before proceeding with fault diagnosis.

As a further illustration of the variations in channel quality, consider the difference between a Western Union teletype system and an online banking system. Occasional misspelling of words in a telegram does not drastically affect the message content. But errors in the online banking system may be intolerable, and more stringent control of the channel parameters is required. The online banking customer ordinarily leases a higher-quality line.

This section is designed to assist in interpreting channel specifications. All of the specified parameters have been discussed in previous sections. They are presented here in condensed form for the purpose of illustrating normal channel tolerances and variations in conditioning.

The circuit specifications discussed are selected as examples only. They should not be construed to be the current offering of any telephone company. However, because of similar requirements of data subscribers, the majority of voice-band channel offerings will be similar in most respects.

Most telephone companies specify their circuit parameters in five categories patterned after the American Telephone and Telegraph Company approach. These categories include circuit designation, general characteristics, attenuation characteristics, delay characteristics, and noise characteristics.

CIRCUIT DESIGNATIONS

The circuit designation is a code name or number used to identify a particular basic channel or conditioning. The use of the circuit is associated with the designation. For example, a particular basic channel may be designated as type 4A, 4B, 4C, and so on as available conditioning.

Another specification may be for a 3002 basic channel with type-C conditioning. Some common uses for which special conditioning normally is used are: data only, voice only, alternate voice and data, teletype, telephoto, and fascimile. An "alternate voice and data or data only" channel is more common in EDP applications.

GENERAL CHARACTERISTICS

The general-characteristic specifications are related to the characteristics of the terminations and permissible connections. Included in this section are the type of service, mode of operation, method and impedance of the terminations, and maximum signal-power levels.

The type of service is described as point-to-point or multipoint. The rates vary for multipoint circuits depending on the number of terminations provided, and in both types of circuits according to the locations of and distance between terminations.

The operational mode may be specified as half- or full-duplex. Simplex applications (one direction only) normally use a half-duplex line. Business machine data communications generally require at least a half-duplex capability.

The method of termination describes the number of wires provided at the subscriber location. Simplex or half-duplex circuits normally have 2-wire terminations. Full-duplex circuits normally have 4-wire terminations. Full-duplex operation is possible with 2-wire terminations.

Also included under general characteristics is a statement of the source and load impedance. A typical specification might read "600 ohms, resistive, balanced." While this is most common, specifications in some countries may be for 500-, 900-, or 1000-ohm circuits and for balanced or unbalanced terminations.

The maximum signal-power level which the subscriber is permitted to apply to the circuit is specified. The amount varies considerably with telephone company, channel type and application. For example, the specification for a 4B data channel may be -8 dbm or -8 VU while the maximum signal power level with type-C conditioning may be 0 dbm or 0 VU (VU is volume units, the equivalent for voice signals to dbm for data signals). A typical maximum power level specification in some overseas areas is −10 dbm or −13 dbm if reverse channel is used.

The maximum signal-power level specification is important to the subscriber, particularly if he supplies the MODEMS. Generally speaking, increasing the transmit power level will result in improved channel operation, better signal-to-noise ratio, and fewer errors. However, exceeding this specification may cause crosstalk and distortion, and at least is not conducive to good relations with the telephone company.

ATTENUATION CHARACTERISTICS

The third category of specifications describe the normal attenuation and frequency attenuation of the channel, and the expected variations in these parameters. A frequency error specification is often included if there are carrier systems involved.

The normal attenuation is specified in dbm. A typical statement may read "8 db ± 1 db at 1000 Hz." The circuit is usually adjusted upon installation to have the correct amount of attenuation. If the circuit is described as above, and if the normal input signal power level is -8 dbm, the received signal power level is probably to be in the range of -15 to -17 dbm [(-8) + (-8±1)]. This situation is illustrated in figure L-1.

In most cases the maximum signal-power level minus the normal attenuation characteristic produces the expected range of receive levels. Another example is similar to C-type conditioning. If the maximum signal-power level is 0 dbm and the normal attenuation is 16 ± 1 db, the expected received level is in the range of -15 to -17 dbm [(0) + (-16±1)].

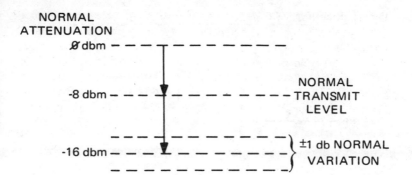

Fig. L-1   Normal attenuation characteristic

The normal attenuation discussed above is accurate only when the circuit is installed. The circuits are adjusted at that time to provide the required amount of normal attenuation. Since the circuits are not monitored continuously, normal variations in circuit gain can be expected over a period of time. These are generally separated according to short- and long-term variations.

Short-term variations are those which occur between telephone company maintenance periods. Long-term variations are those expected to occur because of seasonal changes, circuit aging, and so forth. A typical specification may read: "Expected maximum variation of loss (L) - short term (±3db), long term (±4db)." The expected range of received levels is greater when the measurements are performed some time after the circuit is initially conditioned. Figure L-2 illustrates the expected range of receive levels when the maximum signal power level is -8 dbm, the normal attenuation is 8 ± 1 db, and the short term variation is ±3 dbm.

As illustrated in figure L-2, at the instant of measurement (when the correct input level and frequency is applied) the output level from the circuit may be anywhere in the range of -12 to -20 dbm. When the long-term variation is considered, the range of the output level may vary between -11 and -21 dbm. This is a completely normal situation. In specifying the normal attenuation and expected maximum variations, the telephone company is stating that it will

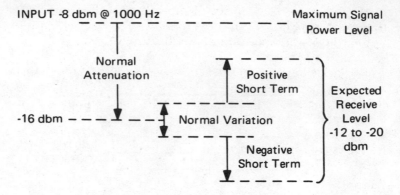

Fig. L-2   Expected variations in channel attenuation

provide the receiving subscriber with an output signal power level in this range if the stated input signal power level is applied to the circuit.

Another specification in this category is the frequency attenuation or frequency response of the channel. This is generally stated as an expected variation of (L) for a change in transmitted frequency over a portion of the channel bandwidth. A typical frequency-response specification might read as follows.

Frequency Range (Hz)	Variation (db)
300-499 (L)	-2 to +6
500-2800 (L)	-1 to +3
2801-3000 (L)	-2 to +6

Since (L) is the net loss measured relative to the loss at 1000 Hz, the frequency-response specification indicates the total range of expected receive levels for any frequency between 300 and 3000 Hz compared to the 1000 Hz reference. Generally, a specification over a wider range of frequencies or a smaller variation over the same range of frequencies represents an improvement in channel quality. As far as data transmission is concerned, the area of interest is that which includes the mark and space frequencies. Ideally, both are received at the same level. At a given measurement time, a difference in receive level between the mark and space frequencies of more than 4 dbm indicates that the channel does not meet the -1 to +3 db specification in the frequency range between 500 and 2800 Hz.

When carrier systems are used, the maximum amount of frequency error introduced by these systems should be specified. Specifications of ±5 or ±10 Hz are common. If the specification is ±10 Hz, 1200 Hz applied to the transmit termination is received as 1200 ± 10 Hz. A 2200 Hz space frequency applied to the same termination is received as 2200 ±10 Hz.

DELAY CHARACTERISTICS

A fourth category of specifications indicates the delay characteristics which the circuit exhibits over the channel bandwidth. For reasons discussed earlier, the absolute delay (delay distortion) is seldom specified. Envelope-delay distortion is specified, however, because it can be readily measured and corrected.

A typical envelope-delay distortion characteristic might be specified as follows.

Frequency range	Envelope delay
1,000 - 2,600 Hz	less than 500 microseconds
600 - 2,600 Hz	less than 1,500 microseconds
500 - 2,800 Hz	less than 3,000 microseconds

Again, a general statement can be made about the characteristic. A broader frequency range for the same amount of delay, or a smaller amount of delay over the same frequency range represents an improvement in channel quality. Envelope-delay specifications are guaranteed parameters or worst-case conditions. A normal channel has somewhat less envelope- delay than the amount specified. Since typical mark and space frequencies are within the 1000- to 2600-Hz range specified above, the remainder of the specification may be ignored for data transmission. Also, reducing the stated specification of envelope-delay distortion in the frequency range of interest should result in improvements as far as delay distortion of the data signals is concerned.

NOISE CHARACTERISTICS

The final category of specifications usually indicates the expected maximum circuit-noise readings. Two types of noise specifications, circuit (random) and impulse noise, are included.

Circuit noise may be stated in dbm, dbrn, or dba. Specifications in dba are less common. They are similar to specifications in dbrn except that the reference is -85 dbm instead of -90 dbm, and a different filter applies to the measurement. A typical circuit noise specification may read:

54 dbrnC0
(26 db)

The "C0" part of the specification indicates a C message filter must be used and the reading is based on 0 dbm. In this case the noise level should cause a maximum reading on a dbm meter (without signal) of -36 dbm (90 - 54 dbrn).

The second part of the specification is the equivalent snr specification in dbm. Given a maximum circuit-noise level of 54 dbrnC0, the ratio of signal-plus-noise/noise should be 26 db or greater.

A signal to noise ratio of 26 db indicates that the nominal aggregate of the signal waveform should be 26 db above the worst-case noise level during transmission. With a normal transmit level of -8 dbm and a noise level of -36 dbm, the snr is 28 db. When insertion loss (normal attenuation at the receiving location) and normal variations are considered, the actual snr at the receive terminals may be worse without exceeding the specification.

Another approach to listing the circuit noise objective is based on circuit length. Table L-1 illustrates typical expected circuit noise readings versus circuit length of an alternate voice and data circuit.

166

Circuit Length (miles)	Expected Noise (dbrnC0)
up to 50	27
50 - 100	30
100 - 200	33
200 - 400	36
400 - 1000	38
1000 - 1500	40
1500 - 2500	42
2500 - 4000	43
4000 - 8000	45

*Data only −54 dbrnC0 if removal of companders is necessary for data operation.

Table L-1   Typical circuit-noise objective

Due to the nature and format of data signals, large amounts of random circuit noise can be tolerated. Impulse noise, however, approximates data signals, and small increases rapidly degrade a data communications system.

A typical impulse noise specification may read:

90 counts in 1/2 hour
@ 68 dbrn0 6A-VB

This specification indicates that a maximum of 90 counts is permissible in a 30-minute period when measured with a Western Electric type 6A or equivalent impulse-noise counter. The threshold of the test set is adjusted to 68 dbrn0 and the VB indicates a voice-band filter is used in the measurement. As far as noise is concerned, the voice-band filter is approximately equivalent to a C message filter.

Noise characteristics may also be used to compare the quality of circuits. Generally, a decrease of circuit noise in dbrn or an increase in the snr in dbm indicates a higher quality circuit. For impulse noise, reducing the number of counts per given amount of time or obtaining the same number of counts for a lower setting of the threshold adjustment (in dbrn) indicates a higher quality circuit.

The importance of basing decisions about circuit quality on *measured* parameters cannot be overemphasized. It is equally important to know the circuit specifications when deciding whether or not a circuit is acceptable. Usually, at least one of the circuit parameters is far outside specifications before the circuit is unacceptable for data transmission.

SUMMARY

This section has presented some typical circuit specifications and their meaning. The local telephone company should be contacted before working on an online system for the technician to become aware of the various channel offerings and the specifications for each.

QUESTIONS

Answers to the following questions are listed in Appendix III.

1. What five categories are normally included in telephone circuit specifications?

2. List some uses of telephone circuits which normally require special conditioning.

3. What specifications generally describe the characteristics of the terminations and permissible connections?

4. If the maximum signal power level is -10 dbm and the normal attenuation is 6 ± 1 dbm, the expected receive level is _____ _ _____ dbm.

5. Why are short-term variations of normal attenuation expected?

6. What is the normal reference for specifications of frequency response?

7. Given two sets of channel frequency response specifications as follows, which channel should provide higher quality data transfer?

Channel A		Channel B	
Freq. Range	Var. (db)	Freq. Range	Var. (db)
350-2000 (L)	-2 to +6	300-499 (L)	-2 to +6
2001-2500 (L)	-3 to +8	500-2400 (L)	-1 to +3
		2401-2700 (L)	-2 to +6

8. What segment of the voice-channel bandwidth is of interest when considering the envelope delay distortion specification as it relates to data transmission?

9. Given two sets of channel envelope delay specifications as follows, which channel should provide higher quality data transfer?

Channel A		Channel B	
Freq. Range	Env. Delay	Freq. Range	Env. Delay
800-2800 Hz	less than 500 us	1000-2600 Hz	less than 500 us

10. A circuit noise specification of 45 dbrn C0 indicates that the maximum amount of noise measured at the receive termination of the circuit with C message weighting is _____ dbm.

11. Given two sets of impulse noise specifications as follows, which channel should provide higher quality data transfer?

Channel A   Channel B

90 counts in 1/2 hour   90 counts in 1/2 hour
@68 dbrn0 6A-VB   @72 dbrn0 6A-VB

Modems in Data Transmission

In the past nearly all telephone companies which provided service to data subscribers also provided MODEMS used in the circuit. In most countries outside of the United States, this is still common practice. Within the United States, telephone company MODEMS are usually required in circuits which access the public switched network, but customer-owned data sets may be used in dedicated circuits when access to the public switched network is impossible.

In a data circuit, there is a physical point of connection between subscriber and telephone company equipment. This point is called the "interface." The technician's area of troubleshooting and maintenance responsibility ends at the interface. The segment of the circuits between interfaces is the responsibility of the telephone company; technicians do not troubleshoot or maintain circuits between interfaces. Also, when the telephone company provides the MODEMS, troubleshooting and maintaining them is not the EDP technician's responsibility and he is usually forbidden by law to do so.

The development of voltage and current protection circuits and other factors are contributing to more permissive attitudes on the part of many telephone companies. New equipment is being designed and manufactured which has MODEMS incorporated as part of the system, and which may use leased telephone circuits on in-house circuits. Systems will be used in the near future in which the MODEMS are the technician's responsibility, and technicians now discuss problems with telephone-company personnel which require knowledge of MODEM functions and operation. This section presents some basic considerations regarding the function, operation, wiring, and testing of MODEMS.

BASIC MODEM CHARACTERISTICS

MODEMS are produced by many manufacturers. In most

cases each manufacturer provides several different models. Individual MODEMS are designed for specific applications and have limited capabilities. The features incorporated into one MODEM may make it desirable for some applications but undesirable for other applications.

Similar MODEMS are usually used at all terminations within a communications circuit because of compatability problems which can arise when different brands or models are used.

In its most basic form, a MODEM is composed of three major sections: a power supply, a transmitter, and a receiver. The power supply provides correct a.c. and d.c. voltages to operate the MODEM circuitry. The transmitter is composed of a modulator and associated amplifier, filter, waveshaping, and level-control circuits. The modulator is the functional section of the transmitter which converts a d.c. data levels to mark and space audio tones. The receiver contains a demodulator circuit which functions in a reverse manner. It converts the mark and space frequencies to corresponding d.c. data levels. Special circuits are also used in the receiver for amplifying, filtering, and shaping the waveforms and controlling signal levels. Figure M-1 illustrates a typical MODEM block diagram showing the basic function.

In figure M-1, data levels are changed to a form which operates the modulator circuit. The output signal from the modulator is an FSK waveform, but it contains many harmonics. (The multivibrator normally used as a transmit oscillator generates the fundamental mark and space frequencies, but the waveforms are distorted.) The transmit

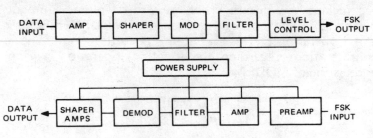

Fig. M-1   Basic MODEM block diagram

filter removes these harmonics and the output waveform is nearly sinusoidal. Level-control circuitry is usually variable in steps to ensure that the correct transmit level is applied to the telephone line at the send terminals. Typical output level controls are variable in 1-, 2-, or 4-dbm steps through the range of 0 dbm to -16 dbm.

The receiver input signal from the telephone line is small in amplitude, typically -12 to -20 dbm. The preamplifier and amplifier circuits raise the signal-power level, and the bandpass filter restricts passage of noise frequencies outside the bandwidth of the mark and space frequencies. Narrowing the bandwidth effectively improves the snr. The demodulator responds to the mark and space frequencies, producing corresponding d.c. data levels as output signals. A shaping circuit is generally used to restore symmetry and squareness (sharp leading and trailing edges) of the data signals. Amplifier circuits then change the d.c. levels to sufficient values required to operate the business machines.

In practice, many additional circuits and signals may be incorporated into the MODEM. These control and supervisory signals fall into two categories: (1) those which are used to cause operations in the MODEM, and (2) those which inform the business machine of conditions in the MODEM or the communications circuit.

Figure M-2 illustrates the most common input, output, and control signals of a MODEM. Many others may be required in different MODEMS, depending upon the design, application, and characteristics of the MODEM. Recommendation V-24 of the CCITT describes the parameters and functions of 29 interface circuits. Most MODEMS have some of these circuits incorporated. The particular circuits included in a MODEM are optional by the manufacturer.

The modulator in figure M-2 is not operational until a "request to send" (RQS) level is provided from the business machine. This voltage enables the transmit oscillator to operate, providing a carrier output waveform (usually the space-frequency signal) to the telephone circuit. A detector circuit recognizes that the transmit oscillator is operational

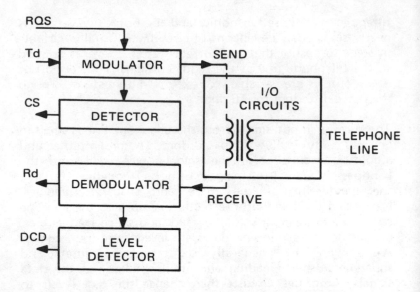

Fig. M-2   Control signal functional diagram

and provides a d.c. level called "clear to send" (CS) to the business machine. CS informs the business machine that the MODEM is ready. The business machine then applies "transmit data" (Td) to the MODEM, and the MODEM converts it to FSK signals. The CS level may be direct or delayed. CS is commonly delayed in the order of 100 to 200 ms to permit the telephone line and equipment to stabilize and to permit the receiving terminal to prepare for receiving the data.

When FSK signals are being received from the telephone circuit, they are applied to the demodulator circuit. If CS is delayed at the transmit MODEM, the carrier (2200 Hz) is being transmitted for a period of time preceding data transfer. During this time, the presence of the carrier in the demodulator circuit is recognized by a level detector which provides a "data carrier detect" (DCD) output level to the business machine. The presence of DCD at the business machine indicates that data transfer is about to take place, and the terminal then performs any operations or functions necessary to condition it to accept the data signals.

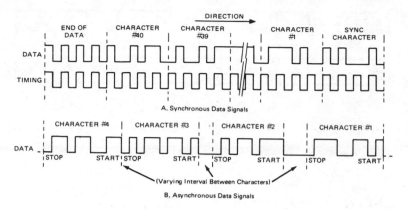

Fig. M-3   Data-signal formats, synchronous and asynchronous modes

MODES OF OPERATION

MODEMS may be designed for synchronous, asynchronous, serial, or parallel transmission. Synchronous and asynchronous refer to the data formats and timing. "Serial" and "parallel" refer to the method of transfer through the communications circuit.

Higher data transfer rates (not transmission speeds) may be obtained by using synchronous transmission. Start and stop bits are *not* transmitted with each character. Groups or blocks of characters are transmitted one after another and individual characters are identified according to the time period which they occupy and their relationship to a timing signal. The timing signal is transmitted simultaneously with the synchronous data characters. Since time is not consumed in the transmission of start and stop bits, faster throughput (data transfer rates) can be obtained.

Asynchronous data transmission is slower but does not require transmission of a separate timing signal. The presence of a start bit indicates to the receiving terminal that a character follows, and a stop bit indicates that the character is complete. Improved error control can be obtained by inserting parity-check bits at the end of each character.

175

BITS	1	2	3	4	TIMING	5	6	7	8
MARK	730	900	1070	1240	1410	1580	1750	1920	2090
SPACE	800	970	1140	1310	1480	1650	1820	1990	2160

Table M-1   Parallel transfer frequencies

The parity bit is added before the character is transmitted. When the receiving terminal checks the parity bit, it immediately detects whether an error has occurred and can arrange for retransmission of that character. Error checks in synchronous transmission occur at the end of a block of characters and error control, and retransmission must wait until the block is completed. Figure M-3 illustrates the difference in format between characters which are transmitted in the synchronous and asynchronous modes.

Serial transmission is the type which has been referred to throughout this text. The characters in a message follow one another. Bits and characters are not transmitted simultaneously but are applied to the circuit in a predetermined sequence.

In parallel transmission two or more bits are transmitted at the same time. Two methods of parallel transmission are possible. One method provides more than one channel and applies data characters (or bits) to separate wires or lines. A second method uses a combination of many frequencies in one channel to represent different bits of simultaneously transmitted characters. The first method is not economical. The second is relatively slow because parallel data sets in current use are incapable of high speed responses from the combination of frequencies in the circuit. NCR uses the second method for some applications. Typical frequencies are shown in table M-1.

This parallel transmission method offers an advantage of reduced interface cost. This results because parallel-to-serial conversion is not necessary and a timing output is provided to the business machine.

REVERSE CHANNEL

An error-control feature often incorporated into MODEMS is called "reverse channel." It provides for the simultaneous transfer over a 2-wire, half-duplex line the data and supervisory (error-control) signals, each being transferred in the opposite direction and not interfering with the other. Data is transferred in the forward direction at the normal rate of 600 or 1200 baud. If an error is detected at the

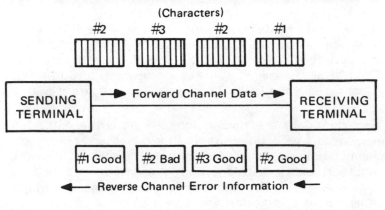

Fig. M-4   Basic reverse channel concept

receive terminal, it uses the reverse channel to inform the sending terminal that an error has occurred and retransmission of the defective character or group of characters is arranged.

Figure M-4 illustrates that data characters pass through the forward channel at the normal rate and that reverse channel information does not require transmission at a high rate. It requires only one "bit" to indicate whether the received data character is acceptable. In figure M-4 character 1 is first to be received. During the time that character 2 is being received, the reverse channel indicates that character 1 is acceptable at the receiving terminal. When character 2 is received, an error is detected. While character 3 is being received, the reverse channel changes condition indicating that character 2 is not correct. Character 3 is received normally, and the reverse channel indicates during the next character time that it did not incur an error. In the meantime, the error indication representing character 2 is recognized by the sending terminal and causes the sending business machine to schedule retransmission of an appropriate part of the message. The part of the message retransmitted includes the character in which the error occurred. Subsequent data characters follow. This example is one of various retransmission schemes using the reverse channel.

The reverse channel makes use of a low-frequency portion of the voice channel bandwidth for a separate FSK signal. Mark and space data signals are centered around 1700 Hz and occupy approximately a 1 kHz segment of the channel. The reverse channel FSK signals occupy a bandwidth of 60 Hz centered around 420 Hz as illustrated in figure M-5.

Two conditions are possible concerning errors. Either an error occurs or it does not. If an error occurs, the reverse channel changes condition from the normal to the error condition and back to the normal condition at a 75-baud rate. The change in frequency is detected by the sending apparatus, and retransmission is scheduled.

The reverse and data channels are combined for transmission and separated after transmission by bandpass filters in the MODEMS. Both channels are present on the line at the same time. The direction of information flow is controlled by the location and frequency response of the filters as illustrated in figure M-6.

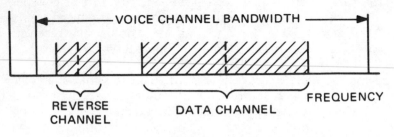

Fig. M-5   Location of the reverse and data channels

It is obvious that both MODEMS in a point-to-point system must contain reverse channel circuitry to produce error control in this manner. Another consideration when reverse channel is used is whether there are echo suppressors in the circuit. In overseas areas 2-wire subscriber lines are usually converted to 4-wire trunk lines. The presence of echo suppressors in the 4-wire trunk inhibits the flow of supervisory data unless the echo suppressor is disabled. This is usually done by transmitting a pure 2100-Hz tone at a level of −13 dbm for at least 300 msec. prior to data transfer. The echo suppressors remain disabled as long as data transfer is continuous. Interrupting the data for a period exceeding 100 msec, causes the echo suppressors to become operational again, and subsequent use of the reverse channel is impossible until the 2100-Hz conditioning tone is retransmitted.

MODEM TESTING AND TROUBLESHOOTING

Most MODEMS incorporate a number of testing, troubleshooting, and conditioning features which improve versatility and reduce maintenance time. The more common features occur in three categories: strapping options, test points, and test modes.

"Strapping" is a term which refers to removable jumpers. These can be connected to different terminals to change the characteristics of the MODEM. The most common strapping options are listed below.

1. Power supply - 120- or 240-volt operation

2. Transmission mode - 2 or 4 wire, half or full duplex

3. Transmission rate - may be selectable

4. Clear to send - direct or delayed

5. Data carrier detect - direct or delayed

6. Reverse channel - may be strapped out

7. Synchronous/asynchronous - may be optional

Test points are usually located at various points in the MODEM for checking the operation of the MODEM circuits and the quality of the input and output waveforms. External test jacks are often provided for observing the send and receive (square) data waveforms and send and receive FSK waveforms. Most often, the data signals are observed and evaluated using an oscilloscope, and FSK waveforms are measured with a dbm meter (transmit and receive levels, snr, etc.). Transmit- and receive-level adjustments may be external or internal, and may be pushbutton switches, rotating selector switches, or strapping options.

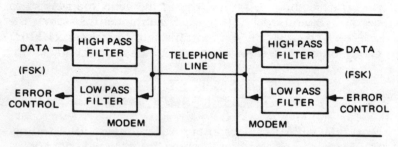

Fig. M-6   Combining the reverse and forward channels

The MODEMS may have optional test modes incorporated to facilitate fault isolation in the system. Two common test modes are the "local test" and the "remote test". Pressing pushbutton switches or changing strapping jumpers may place the MODEM in a test mode. The exact method varies with manfuacturers.

The local test mode is used to check the operation of the local MODEM. The business machine remains connected to the MODEM during this test. Control levels from the business machine operate the MODEM and normal data signals are used for testing.

Figure M-7 illustrates signal flow in the local-test mode. RQS and Td from the business machine operate the transmitter in the MODEM. The data levels are converted to FSK signals. Instead of being applied to the telephone line, they are attenuated a normal amount and applied to the receiver in the same MODEM. The FSK signals are converted to data signals in the receiver, and the send and receive data signals (Td and Rd) should be identical waveforms (except for absolute delay differences). Drastic differences in data waveforms or the absence of data at Rd indicates a failure in the MODEM.

The remote-test feature is similar but includes the telephone line and remote MODEM in the circuit. The signal flow in the remote-test mode is illustrated in figure M-8.

After the local test proves that MODEM 1 is operational, it is again connected to the telephone circuit. MODEM 2 is placed in the remote configuration. Data is converted to FSK signals by MODEM 1, transmitted through the circuit, and received by MODEM 2. The receiver converts the FSK signals to data which is applied directly to the transmitter in MODEM 2 and retransmitted in the opposite direction over a separate line. The MODEM 1 receiver produces DCD and Rd if the loop is complete. As before, comparison of Td and Rd waveforms indicate whether there is a failure in the circuit.

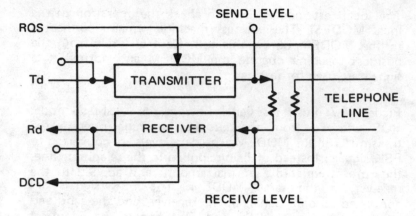

Fig. M-7   Local-test mode

If the local test proves MODEM 1 operates correctly but errors occur in the remote test, then either the telephone circuit or MODEM 2 is at fault. Use of the business machine and local-test modes at MODEM 2 (the remote site) may indicate that MODEM 2 is not operational and requires corrective maintenance. If both MODEM 1 and MODEM 2 operate satisfactorily in the local-test modes but not in the remote test mode, one of the telephone circuits is *probably* at fault.

Local and remote tests are useful in the system approach to fault diagnosis. Performing the local and remote tests *usually* indicates which segment of the circuit is at fault. But the problem is more difficult when two or more segments provide marginal operation. For example, if the two MODEMS are improperly adjusted, each may operate in the local mode but degrade the system sufficiently when connected together to cause errors. A telephone line with marginal attenuation combined with improperly adjusted transmit- or receive-level attenuators in a MODEM may produce the same effect. Proper adjustment of the level attenuator will not "fix" the telephone circuit, but may make the situation acceptable.

Proper use of the local- and remote-test modes and test points can considerably reduce the time required for fault diagnosis. External test points for measuring transmit and receive FSK levels are usually provided. It is good practice to measure the transmit and receive levels as a matter of course and to make any required adjustments to the transmit and receive level attenuators.

It is worth restating that MODEMS which are leased from the telephone-company are *not* the technician's responsibility. He should not make adjustments to or perform measurements in telephone-company equipment without permission of the company. If he obtains permission to measure transmit and receive levels at the MODEM, he should use caution to prevent damage to the equipment. If MODEM failure is indicated, he should coordinate repair or replacement with the telephone company.

Most MODEMS are transistorized and contain modular plug-in circuit boards. The quickest method of restoring a defective MODEM to operation is to replace the defective circuit board. The following example illustrates an efficient approach to fault diagnosis and circuit isolation which may be used with our MODEMS. Assume that the MODEM is

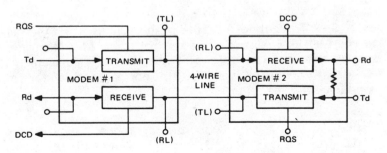

Fig. M-8 Remote-test mode

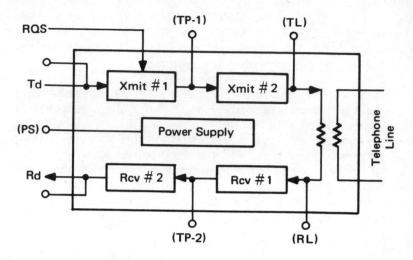

Fig. M-9   Sample MODEM block diagram and test points

connected to an operational business machine and is in the
local test mode. As shown in figure M-9, assume that two
circuit boards are used in the transmitter, two in the
receiver, and one in the power supply. Test points include
RQS, Td, transmit oscillator output (TP-1), transmit level
(TL), receive level (RL), demodulator output (TP-2), Rd,
and a power supply test jack (PS).

If RQS or Td is abnormal, the problem is usually external
to the MODEM. If these are normal, table M-2 illustrates
step-by-step approach to circuit isolation and replacement.
N and A are used to indicate normal and abnormal
conditions.

Table M-2 illustrates a sequential approach, following the
signal from test point to test point until an abnormal
indication is obtained. Another technique called "split
half" divides the group of circuits approximately in half.

The first measurement at that point (TL or RL) indicates
which half of the circuits are at fault. A normal
measurement indicates that all preceding circuits are

	(TP-1)	(TL)	(RL)	(TP-2)	Rd	(PS)	Replace or Test
C O N D I T I O N	A					A	Power Supply
	A					N	Xmit #1
	N	A				N	Xmit #2
	N	N	A			N	Local Test Sw.
	N	N	N	A		N	Rcv #1
	N	N	N	N	A	N	Rcv #2

Table   M-2   Test-point indications

operational. The remainder of the circuits are split in half again. In the example, this would be TP-2. If the MODEM is not operational in the beginning, normal measurement at TP-2 indicates that RCV has failed. An abnormal measurement at TP-2 indicates RCV 1 is faulty (all preceding circuits were checked with the first measurement).

SUMMARY

The most important point in this chapter is the definition of the technicians area of troubleshooting and maintenance responsibility. When dealing with the area between interfaces he should proceed cautiously, taking care to tactfully coordinate with the telephone company for the resolution of circuit problems.

When the MODEMS *are* the technician's responsibility, he has considerably more freedom in approach. He may use local and remote tests and test points freely to isolate the trouble to a part of the system. He should develop logical, sequential approaches to system and circuit troubleshooting which produces the defective circuit in the least amount of time.

QUESTIONS

Answers to the following questions are listed in Appendix III.

1. At what physical point in an online system does the EDP technician's troubleshooting and maintenance responsibility end?

2. What three major sections are included in a MODEM?

3. Which section of the MODEM converts mark and space FSK frequencies to d.c. mark and space levels?

4. Will the modulator section of the MODEM be operational if the "request to send" (RQS) line from the business machine is open?

5. What causes a "data carrier detect" (DCD) level to be generated by a MODEM?

6. What is one advantage of synchronous transmission compared to asynchronous transmission?

7. Why are parity bits added to data characters?

8. When do error checks occur in synchronous transmission?

9. What prevents the reverse-channel information from interfering with the forward-channel information when both are present on the same 2-wire line?

10. Why must echo suppressors be disabled during reverse-channel operation?

11. What is meant by "strapping"?

12. What equipment may be checked when a MODEM is in a local-test mode?

13. What equipment may be checked when a MODEM is in a remote test mode?

14. What is usually the quickest method of restoring a defective MODEM to operation?

15. Should an EDP technician make measurements or adjustments in equipment which is leased from the telephone company?

Final Exam

Answers to the following questions are listed in Appendix III.

1. The technique of transposing channels to different locations in a spectrum and then combining them, through hybrid circuits, for simultaneous transmission is called:

   a. Modulating.
   b. Frequency division multiplexing.
   c. Heterodyning.
   d. Time division multiplexing.

2. A circuit designed to attenuate all frequencies except those that fall between 16kHz and 20kHz is referred to as a:

   a. Band pass filter.
   b. Band reject filter.
   c. High pass filter.
   d. Low pass filter.

3. A steady signal of −3dbm would appear as an oscilloscope reading of:

   a. 0.55 volts rms.
   b. 0.55 volts pk-pk.
   c. 0.55 volts DC.
   d. 1.55 volts pk-pk.
   e. 1.55 volts rms.

4. High amplitude peaks that exceed a predetermined level and appear in the noise waveform of a communication channel are identified as:

   a. White noise.
   b. Hits.
   c. Impulse noise.
   d. Echoes.
   e. Random noise.

5. A method of information transfer in which each bit of a character follows the preceding bits of that character is called:

   a. Synchronous transmission.
   b. Asynchronous transmission.
   c. Serial transmission.
   d. Parallel transmission.

6. The bandpass of the telephone company voice grade channel is:

   a. 3200 Hz.
   b. 200 Hz. − 3200 Hz.
   c. 1000 Hz.
   d. 1200 Hz. − 2200 Hz.
   e. 3000 Hz.

7. If the signal level being received was −17dbm and the circuit noise level was 40 dbrn, the signal to noise ratio would be:

   a. 23 db.

   b. 57db.
   c. 33db.
   d. 67db.
   e. 73db.

8. Which one of the following output signals would be produced by a negative input to a modem?

   a. A 2200 Hz. "mark" signal.
   b. A 2200 Hz. "space" signal.
   c. A 1200 Hz. "space" signal.
   d. A 1200 Hz. "mark" signal.

9. An "on-line" system where each remote location will have its own full-time circuit to the central processor will require:

   a. Point-to-point, dedicated line service.
   b. Multi-point, public switched service.
   c. Multi-point, dedicated line service.
   d. Point-to-point, public switched service.

10. The method of referencing transmitted data by "framing" each character with start and stop bits is called:

   a. Synchronous transmission.
   b. Asynchronous transmission.
   c. Serial transmission.
   d. Parallel transmission.

11. A transmission problem that results in signals of one frequency being reduced in amplitude more than signals of another frequency is called:

   a. Attenuation.
   b. Envelope delay.
   c. Attenuation frequency distortion.
   d. Delay distortion.
   e. Attenuation distortion.

12. The remote terminal is transmitting a 1kHz signal measured at .22 volts rms. The signal received at the processor is measured with an oscilloscope at .22 volts pk-pk. The end to end circuit shows:

   a. A loss of 2dbm.
   b. A gain of 9dbm.
   c. No power loss or gain.
   d. A loss of 9dbm.
   e. A loss of 11dbm.

13. The standard interface term, sent from a business machine to its modem, that enables the oscillator to turn on is called:

   a. Transmit data.
   b. Clear to send.

c. Request to send.
d. Reverse channel.
e. Data carrier detect.

14. Given the following envelope delay specifications, which channel should give the highest quality service if FSK signals of 1200Hz and 2200Hz are used for data transfer?

		Frequency Range (Hz)	Envelope Delay
a.	Channel A	1000-2400	Less than 2000 μ Sec.
b.	Channel B	1000-2400	Less than 1500 μ Sec.
c.	Channel C	1000-2400	Less than 1000 μ Sec.
d.	Channel D	1000-2400	Less than 2500 μ Sec.
e.	Channel E	1000-2400	Less than 3000 μ Sec.

15. "Balanced" termination refers to a telephone circuit that:

a. Is grounded at both ends.
b. Is not grounded at all.
c. Has both of the subscriber lines grounded.
d. Has one of the subscriber lines grounded.
e. Is grounded at its electrical center.

16. The advantage of the "local test" feature in modem design is that it will permit testing the:

a. Transmitter and receiver.
b. Transmitter only.
c. Transmitter, receiver, and communication lines.
d. Receiver only.
e. Communication lines.

17. The process of changing a DC data signal so it will be suitable for transmission over telephone lines is called:

a. Amplification.
b. Deviation.
c. Multiplexing.
d. Attenuation.
e. Modulation.

18. A delay equalizer is a corrective device that is used in communication circuits to compensate for:

a. Crosstalk.
b. Absolute delay.
c. Attenuation distortion.
d. Delay distortion.
e. Echoes.

19. Normal characteristics of a wired transmission line will cause attenuation of:

a. Lower frequencies more than higher frequencies.
b. Higher frequencies more than lower frequencies.
c. The high frequencies only.
d. The low frequencies only.

20. A business machine circuit that inverts and changes voltage levels of data signals is called a:

a. Level converter.
b. Balanced modulator.
c. Modem.
d. Non-linear mixer.
e. Linear mixer.

21. Given the following frequency response specifications, which channel should give the highest quality service if FSK signals of 1200 Hz. and 2200 Hz. are used for data transfer?

		Frequency Range (Hz)	Variation Of Loss (db)
a.	Channel A	1200-2200	-2 to +8
b.	Channel B	1000-2400	-2 to +8
c.	Channel C	800-2600	-2 to +8
d.	Channel D	600-2800	-2 to +8
e.	Channel E	400-3000	-2 to +8

22. What corrective element in a communication circuit must be disabled by a modem using the reverse channel feature?

a. Compander.
b. Delay equalizer.
c. Repeater.
d. Echo suppressor.
e. Amplifier.

23. A communication mode in which data flow can occur in both directions at the same time is called:

a. Simplex.
b. Full duplex.
c. Half duplex.
d. Duplex.

24. The technique of converting DC data signals to one of two predetermined frequencies is called:

a. Frequency shift keying.
b. Frequency distortion.
c. Frequency division multiplexing.
d. Frequency modulation.
e. Frequency translation.

25. Select the statement that is MOST correct.

a. Impedance of a transmission line section is determined by length.
b. Impedance of a communication circuit is 600 ohms.
c. Impedance of communication circuits will vary with frequency.
d. Attenuation frequency distortion is caused by a circuit that is not impedance matched.
e. Transformers are used for impedance matching because they have no power loss.

Reference Data

USASCII CODE CHART AND ABBREVIATIONS

B_4–B_1 → / B_8–B_5 ↓	0000 0	0001 1	0010 2	0011 3	0100 4	0101 5	0110 6	0111 7	1000 8	1001 9	1010 A	1011 B	1100 C	1101 D	1110 E	1111 F
0000 **0**	NUL	SOH	STX	ETX	EOT	ENQ	ACK	BEL	BS	HT	LF	VT	FF	CR	SO	SI
0001 **1**	DLE	DCI	DC2	DC3	DC4	NAK	SYN	ETB	CAN	EM	SUB	ESC	FS	GS	RS	US
0010 **2**	⊠	!	"	#	$	%	&	'	(	)	*	+	,	-	.	/
0011 **3**	0	1	2	3	4	5	6	7	8	9	:	;	<	=	>	?
0100 **4**	@	A	B	C	D	E	F	G	H	I	J	K	L	M	N	O
0101 **5**	P	Q	R	S	T	U	V	W	X	Y	Z	[	\	]	^	_
0110 **6**	`	a	b	c	d	e	f	g	h	i	j	k	l	m	n	o
0111 **7**	p	q	r	s	t	u	v	w	x	y	z	{	¦	}	~	DEL

Col./Row	Symbol	Name		Control Character	Function
2/0	SP	Space (Normally Non-Printing)		NUL	Null
2/1	!	Exclamation Point		SOH	Start of Heading
2/2	"	Quotation Marks (Diaeresis)		STX	Start of Text
2/3	#	Number Sign		ETX	End of Text
2/4	$	Dollar Sign		EOT	End of Transmission
2/5	%	Percent		ENQ	Enquiry
2/6	&	Ampersand		ACK	Acknowledge
2/7	'	Apostrophe (Closing Single		BEL	Bell (audible or attention signal)
		Quotation Mark ; Acute Accent)		BS	Backspace
2/8	(	Opening Parenthesis		HT	Horizontal Tabulation
2/9	)	Closing Parenthesis			(punched card skip)
2/A	*	Asterisk		LF	Line Feed
2/B	+	Plus		VT	Vertical Tabulation
2/C	,	Comma (Cedilla)		FF	Form Feed
2/D	-	Hyphen (Minus)		CR	Carriage Return
2/E	.	Period (Decimal Point)		SO	Shift Out
2/F	/	Slant		SI	Shift In
3/A	:	Colon		DLE	Data Link Escape
3/B	;	Semicolon		DCI	Device Control 1
3/C	<	Less Than		DC2	Device Control 2
3/D	=	Equals		DC3	Device Control 3
3/E	>	Greater Than		DC4	Device Control 4 (Stop)
3/F	?	Question Mark		NAK	Negative Acknowledge
4/0	@	Commercial At		SYN	Synchronous Idle
5/B	[	Opening Bracket		ETB	End of Transmission Block
5/C	\	Reverse Slant		CAN	Cancel
5/D	]	Closing Bracket		EM	End of Medium
5/E	^	Circumflex		SUB	Substitute
5/F	—	Underline		ESC	Escape
6/0	`	Grave Accent (Opening		FS	File Separator
		Single Quotation Mark)		GS	Group Separator
7/B	{	Opening Brace		RS	Record Separator
7/C	¦	Vertical Line		US	Unit Separator
7/D	}	Closing Brace		DEL	Delete
7/E	~	Overline (Tilde, General Accent)			

USASCII graphic symbols   Control character functions

INTERNATIONAL ALPHABET No. 2 TELETYPE CODE   (BAUDOT)

CHARACTER

UPPER CASE	LOWER CASE	START	BIT 1	BIT 2	BIT 3	BIT 4	BIT 5	STOP
A	.	0	1	1	0	0	0	1
B	?	0	1	0	0	1	1	1
C	:	0	0	1	1	1	0	1
D	$	0	1	0	0	1	0	1
E	3	0	1	0	0	0	0	1
F	!	0	1	0	1	1	0	1
G	&	0	0	1	0	1	1	1
H	£	0	0	0	1	0	1	1
I	8	0	0	1	1	0	0	1
J	'	0	1	1	0	1	0	1
K	(	0	1	1	1	1	0	1
L	)	0	0	1	0	0	1	1
M	.	0	0	0	1	1	1	1
N	,	0	0	0	1	1	0	1
O	9	0	0	0	0	1	1	1
P	0	0	0	1	1	0	1	1
Q	1	0	1	1	1	0	1	1
R	4	0	0	1	0	1	0	1
S	BELL	0	1	0	1	0	0	1
T	5	0	0	0	0	0	1	1
U	7	0	1	1	1	0	0	1
V	;	0	0	1	1	1	1	1
W	2	0	1	1	0	0	1	1
X	/	0	1	0	1	1	1	1
Y	6	0	1	0	1	0	1	1
Z	"	0	1	0	0	0	1	1
BLANK		0	0	0	0	0	0	1
SPACE		0	0	1	0	0	0	1
CR		0	0	0	0	1	0	1
LF		0	0	1	0	0	0	1
UC		0	1	1	0	1	1	1
LC		0	1	1	1	1	1	1

0 = SPACE = NO CURRENT   1 = MARK = CURRENT

WIRE GAUGES REFERENCE

GAUGE NO.	Dia. In.	Bare Wire Mills	Area in Cir Mils (Square of Mils)	Current Capability (Amps) Rubber Ins.	Other Ins.	Ohms/1000 Ft. 70°F.	167°F.
4/0	0.460	460	211,600	160-248	193-510	0.050	0.060
3/0	.410	410	167,800	138-215	166-429	.062	.075
2/0	.365	365	133,100	120-185	145-372	.080	.095
0	.325	325	105,600	105-160	127-325	.100	.119
1	.289	289	83,690	91-136	110-280	.127	.150
2	.258	258	66,560	80-118	96-241	.159	.190
3	.229	229	52,441	69-101	83-211	.202	.240
4	.204	204	41,620	60-87	72-180	.254	.302
5	.182	182	33,120	52-76	63-158	.319	.381
6	.162	162	26,240	45-65	54-134	.403	.480
7	.144	144	20,740	. . . .		.510	.606
8	.128	128	16,380	35-48	41-100	.465	.764
9	.114	114	13,000	. . . .		.813	.963
10	.102	102	10,400	25-35	31-75	1.02	1.216
11	.091	91	8,230	. . . .		1.29	1.532
12	.081	81	6,530	20-26	23-57	1.62	1.931
13	.072	72	5,180	. . . .		2.04	2.436
14	.064	64	4,110	15-20	18-43	2.57	3.071
15	.057	57	3,260	. . . .		3.24	3.873
16	.051	51	2,580	6	10	4.10	4.884
17	.045	45	2,060	. . . .		5.15	6.158
18	.040	40	1,620	3	6	6.51	7.765
19	.036	36	1,290	. . . .		8.21	9.792
20	.032	32	1,020	. . . .		10.3	12.35
21	.028	28	812	. . . .		13.0	15.57
22	.025	25	640	. . . .		16.5	19.63
23	.024	24	511	. . . .		20.7	24.76
24	.020	20	404	. . . .		26.2	31.22
25	.018	18	320	. . . .		33.0	39.36
26	.016	16	253	. . . .		41.8	49.64
27	.014	14	202	. . . .		52.4	62.59
28	.013	13	159	. . . .		66.6	78.93
29	.011	11	128	. . . .		82.8	99.52
31	.009	9	79	. . . .		134.0	158.20
32	.008	8	64	. . . .		165.0	199.50
33	.007	7	50	. . . .		210.0	251.60
34	.006	6	40	. . . .		266.0	317.30
35	.005	5.6	31	. . . .		337.0	400.00
36	.005	5	25	. . . .		423.0	504.50

Approximate Dimensions and Resistances of Commercial Copper Wire: American Standard Wire Gauge.

COMMON LOGARITHMS

N	0	1	2	3	4	5	6	7	8	9
10	0000000	0043214	0086002	0128372	0170333	0211893	0253059	0293838	0334238	0374265
11	0413927	0453230	0492180	0530784	0569049	0606978	0644580	0681859	0718820	0755470
12	0791812	0827854	0863598	0899051	0934217	0969100	1003705	1038037	1072100	1105897
13	1139434	1172713	1205739	1238516	1271048	1303338	1335389	1367206	1398791	1430148
14	1461280	1492191	1522883	1553360	1583625	1613680	1643529	1673173	1702617	1731863
15	1760913	1789769	1818436	1846914	1875207	1903317	1931246	1958997	1986571	2013971
16	2041200	2068259	2095150	2121876	2148438	2174839	2201081	2227165	2253093	2278867
17	2304489	2329961	2355284	2380461	2405492	2430380	2455127	2479733	2504200	2528530
18	2552725	2576786	2600714	2624511	2648178	2671717	2695129	2718416	2741578	2764618
19	2787536	2810334	2833012	2855573	2878017	2900346	2922561	2944662	2966652	2988531
20	3010300	3031961	3053514	3074960	3096302	3117539	3138672	3159703	3180633	3201463
21	3222193	3242825	3263359	3283796	3304138	3324385	3324538	3364597	3384565	3404441
22	3424227	3443923	3463530	3483049	3502480	3521825	3541084	3560259	3579348	3598355
23	3617278	3636120	3654880	3673559	3692159	3710679	3729120	3747483	3765770	3783979
24	3802112	3820170	3838154	3856063	3873898	3891661	3909351	3926970	3944517	3961993
25	3979400	3996737	4014005	4031205	4048337	4065402	4082400	4099331	4116197	4132998
26	4149733	4166405	4183013	4199557	4216039	4232459	4248816	4265113	4281348	4297523
27	4313638	4329693	4345689	4361626	4377506	4393327	4409091	4424798	4440448	4456042
28	4471580	4487063	4502491	4517864	4533183	4548449	4563660	4578819	4593925	4608978
29	4623980	4638930	4653829	4668676	4683473	4698220	4712917	4727564	4742163	4756712
30	4771213	4785665	4800069	4814426	4828736	4842998	4587214	4871384	4885507	4899585
31	4913617	4927604	4941546	4955443	4969296	4983106	4996871	5010593	5024271	5037907
32	5051500	5065050	5078559	5092025	5105450	5118534	5132176	5145478	5158738	5171959
33	5185139	5198280	5211381	5224442	5237465	5250448	5263393	5276299	5289167	5301997
34	5314789	5327544	5340261	5352941	5365584	5378191	5390761	5403295	5415792	5428254
35	5440680	5453071	5465427	5477747	5490033	5502284	5514500	5526682	5538830	5505944
36	5563025	5575072	5587086	5599066	5611014	5622929	5634811	5646661	5658478	5670264
37	5682017	5693739	5705429	5717088	5728716	5740313	5751878	5763414	5774918	5786392
38	5797836	5809250	5820634	5831988	5843312	5854607	5865873	5877110	5888317	5899496
39	5910646	5921768	5932861	5943926	5954962	5965971	5976952	5987905	5998831	6009729
40	6020600	6031444	6042261	6053050	6063814	6074550	6085260	6095944	6106602	6117233
41	6127839	6138418	6148972	6159501	6170003	6180481	6190933	6201361	6211763	6222140
42	6232493	6242821	6253125	6263404	6273659	6283889	6294096	6304279	6314438	6324573
43	6334685	6344773	6354837	6364879	6374897	6384893	6394865	6404814	6414741	6424645
44	6434527	6444386	6454223	6464037	6473830	6483600	6493349	6503075	6512780	6522463
45	6532125	6541765	6551384	6560982	6570559	6580114	6589648	6599162	6608655	6618127
46	6627578	6637099	6646420	6655810	6665180	6674530	6683859	6693169	6702459	6711728
47	6720979	6730209	6739420	6748611	6757783	6766936	6776070	6785184	6794279	6803355
48	6812412	6821451	6830470	6839471	6848454	6857417	6866363	6875290	6884198	6893089
49	6901961	6910815	6919651	6928469	6937269	6946052	6954817	6963564	6972293	6981005
50	6989700	6998377	7007037	7015680	7024305	7032914	7041505	7050080	7058637	7067178
51	7075702	7084209	7092700	7101174	7109631	7118072	7126497	7134905	7143298	7151674
52	7160033	7168377	7176705	7185017	7193313	7201593	7209857	7218106	7226339	7234557
53	7242759	7250945	7259116	7267272	7275413	7283538	7291648	7299743	7307823	7315888
54	7323938	7331973	7339993	7347998	7355989	7363965	7371926	7379873	7387806	7395723
55	7403627	7411516	7419391	7427251	7435098	7442930	7450748	7458552	7466342	7474118
56	7481980	7489629	7497363	7505084	7512791	7520484	7528164	7535831	7543483	7551123
57	7338749	7566361	7573960	7581546	7589119	7596678	7604225	7611758	7619278	7626786
58	7634280	7641761	7649230	7656686	7664128	7671559	7678976	7686381	7693773	7701153
59	7708520	7715875	7723217	7730547	7737864	7745170	7752463	7759743	7767012	7774268
60	7781513	7788745	7795965	7803173	7810369	7817554	7824726	7831887	7839036	7846173
61	7853298	7860412	7867514	7874605	7881684	7888751	7895807	7902852	7909885	7916906
62	7923917	7930916	7937904	7944880	7951846	7958800	7965743	7972675	7979596	7986506
63	7993405	8000294	8007171	8014037	8020893	8027737	8034571	8041394	8048207	8055009
64	8061800	8068580	8075350	8082110	8088859	8095597	8102325	8109043	8115750	8122447
65	8129134	8135810	8142476	8149132	8155777	8162413	8169038	8175654	8182259	8188854
66	8195439	8202015	8208580	8215135	8221681	8228216	8234742	8241258	8247765	8254261
67	8260748	8267225	8273693	8280151	8286599	8293038	8299467	8305887	8312297	8318698
68	8325089	8331471	8337844	8344207	8350561	8356906	8363241	8369567	8375884	8382192
69	8388491	8394780	8401061	8407332	8413505	8419848	8426092	8432328	8438554	8444772
70	8450980	8547180	8463371	8469553	8475727	8481891	8488047	8494194	8500333	8506462
71	8512583	8518696	8524800	8530895	8536982	8543060	8549130	8555192	8561244	8567289
72	8573325	8579353	8585372	8591383	8597386	8603380	8609366	8615344	8621314	8627275
73	8633229	8639174	8645111	8651040	8656961	8662873	8668778	8674675	8680564	8686444
74	8692317	8698182	8704039	8709888	8715729	8721563	8727388	8733206	8739016	8744818
75	8750613	8756399	8762178	8767950	8773713	8779470	8785218	8790959	8796692	8802418
76	8808136	8813847	8819550	8825245	8830934	8836614	8842288	8847954	8853612	8859263
77	8864907	8870544	8876173	8881795	8887410	8893017	8898617	8904210	8909796	8915375
78	8920946	8926510	8932068	8937618	8943161	8948697	8954225	8959747	8965262	8970770
79	8976271	8981765	8987252	8992732	8998205	9003671	9009131	9014583	9020029	9025468

COMMON LOGARITHMS (CONTINUED)

N	0	1	2	3	4	5	6	7	8	9
80	9030900	9036325	9041774	9047155	9052560	9057959	9063350	9068735	9074114	9079485
81	9084850	9090209	9095560	9100905	9106244	9111576	9116902	9122221	9127533	9132839
82	9138139	9143432	9148718	9153998	9159272	9164539	9169800	9175055	9180303	9185545
83	9190781	9196010	9201233	9206450	9211661	9216865	9222063	9227255	9232440	9237620
84	9242793	9247960	9253121	9258276	9263424	9268567	9273704	9278834	9283959	9289077
85	9294189	9299296	9304396	9309490	9314579	9319661	9324738	9329808	9334873	9339932
86	9344985	9350032	9355073	9360108	9365137	9370161	9375179	9380191	9385197	9390198
87	9395193	9400182	9405165	9410142	9415114	9420081	9425041	9429996	9434945	9439889
88	9444827	9449759	9454686	9459607	9464523	9469433	9474337	9479236	9484130	9489018
89	9493900	9498777	9503649	9508515	9513375	9518230	9523080	9527924	9532763	9537597
90	9542425	9547248	9552065	9556878	9561684	9566486	9571282	9576073	9580858	9585639
91	9590414	9595184	9599948	9604708	9609462	9614211	9618955	9623693	9628427	9633155
92	9637878	9642596	9647309	9652017	9656720	9661417	9666110	9670797	9675480	9680157
93	9684829	9689497	9694159	9698816	9703469	9708116	9712758	9717396	9722028	9726656
94	9731279	9735896	9740509	9745117	9749720	9754318	9758911	9763500	9768083	9772662
95	9777236	9781805	9786369	9790929	9795484	9800034	9804579	9809119	9813655	9818186
96	9822712	9827234	9831751	9836263	9840770	9845273	9849771	9854265	9858754	9863238
97	9867717	9872192	9876663	9881128	9885590	9890046	9894498	9898946	9903389	9907827
98	9912261	9916690	9921115	9925535	9929951	9934362	9938769	9943172	9947569	9951963
99	9956352	9960737	9965117	9969492	9973864	9978231	9982593	9986952	9991305	9995655

DBM QUICK CONVERSION CHART

	DBM	RMSV	PPV
+	10	2.45	6.90
	9	2.18	6.18
	8	1.95	5.51
	7	1.74	4.91
	6	1.55	4.38
	5	1.38	3.90
	4	1.23	3.48
	3	1.10	3.10
	2	0.96	2.76
	1	0.87	2.46
	0	0.775	2.19
−	1	0.69	1.96
	2	0.62	1.74
	3	0.55	1.55
	4	0.49	1.38
	5	0.44	1.23
	6	0.39	1.10
	7	0.35	0.98
	8	0.31	0.87
	9	0.27	0.78
	10	0.25	0.69
	11	0.22	0.62
	12	0.19	0.55
	13	0.17	0.49
	14	0.15	0.44
	15	0.14	0.39
	16	0.12	0.35
	17	0.11	0.31
	18	0.10	0.28
	19	0.09	0.25
	20	0.08	0.22
	21	0.07	0.20
	22	0.06	0.17
	23	0.05	0.16
	24	0.05	0.14
	25	0.04	0.12
	26	0.04	0.11
	27	0.03	0.10
	28	0.03	0.09
	29	0.03	0.08
	30	0.02	0.07
	35	0.01	0.04
	40	0.008	0.02
	45	0.004	0.01
	50	0.002	0.007

Table of Equivalence (dbm) for 1 Khz into a 600 ohm line

RATIO-TO-DB QUICK CONVERSION CHART

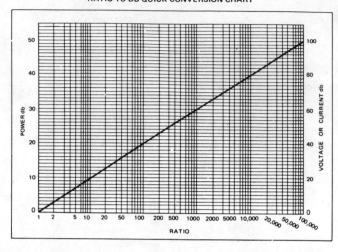

STANDARD INTERFACE CONNECTIONS

		Circuit Name	Direction Mach. ↔ Modem	Function*	EIA
CCITT ckt =	1	Protective ground			AA
	2	Signal ground (common)			AB
	3	Transmitted data	→	DO	BA
	4	Received data	←	DI	BB
	5	Request to Send	→	DO	CA
	6	Ready to Send (CS)	←	DO	CB
	7	Data set ready	←	DO	CC
	8	Connect Data set to line	→	DO	CD
	9	Data Carrier detect	←	DI	CF
	10	Data signal quality	←	DI	CG
	11	Data rate selector	→	SP	CH
	12	Data rate selector	←	SP	CI
	13	Transmitter timing	→	DO	DA
	14	Transmitter timing	←	DO	DB
	15	Receiver timing	←	DI	DD
	16	Trans. block timing	→	DO	
	17	Receiver block timing	←	DI	
	18	Transmitted data (reverse)	→	SDO	
	19	Received data (reverse)	←	SDI	
	20	Transmit carrier	→	SDO	
	21	Supervisor channel ready	←	SDO	
	22	Carrier detect	←	SDI	
	23	Quality detector	←	SDI	
	24	Data receiver cut-off	→	DI	
	25	Calling indicator	←	(signal)	CE
	26	Select trans. frequency	→	DO	
	27	Select receiver frequency	→	DI	
	28	Receiver timing	→	DI	DC
	29	Receiver cut-off	→	SDI	

D	=	Data
I	=	Input
O	=	Output
SP	=	Signalling Speed
S	=	Supervisory

NOTE

Most modems incorporate only the
required functions and signals, the others
being ignored.

REFERENCE DATA · FORMULAS

CONSTANTS

$$\pi = 3.14$$
$$\sqrt{2} = 1.414$$
$$1 \text{ Meter} = 39.37 \text{ in.}$$
$$\frac{1}{2\pi} = .159$$

OHMS LAW · DC

$$I = \frac{E}{R}$$
$$E = IR$$
$$R = \frac{E}{I}$$
$$P = I^2 R = EI = \frac{E^2}{R}$$

OHMS LAW · AC

$$I = \frac{E}{Z}$$
$$E = IZ$$
$$Z = \frac{E}{I}$$

RESISTORS · SERIES

$$R \text{ total} = R_1 + R_2 + R_3 \ldots$$

RESISTORS · PARALLEL

$$R \text{ total} = \frac{1}{\left(\frac{1}{R_1} + \frac{1}{R_2} + \frac{1}{R_3} \ldots\right)}$$

TWO RESISTORS · PARALLEL

$$R \text{ total} = \frac{R_1 \, R_2}{R_1 + R_2}$$

EQUAL RESISTORS · PARALLEL

$$R \text{ total} = \frac{R}{N}$$

(N = number in parallel)

SINUSOIDAL VOLTAGES · CURRENTS

Effective	=	.707 Peak
Average	=	.637 Peak
Peak	=	1.414 Effective
Peak to Peak	=	2.828 Effective
Effective	=	RMS

REACTANCE FORMULAS

$$X_C = \frac{1}{2\pi f c}$$
$$X_l = 2\pi f l$$
$$L = \frac{X_l}{2\pi f}$$

RESONANCE FORMULAS

$$f = \frac{1}{2\pi \sqrt{LC}} = \frac{.159}{\sqrt{LC}}$$
$$L = \frac{1}{4\pi^2 f^2 C}$$
$$C = \frac{1}{4\pi^2 f^2 L}$$

IMPEDANCE FORMULAS

SERIES CIRCUIT

$$Z = \sqrt{R^2 + (X_l \cdot X_C)^2}$$

PARALLEL CIRCUIT

$$Z = \frac{R_x}{\sqrt{R^2 + X^2}}$$

DECIBEL FORMULAS

EQUAL IMPEDANCES

$$db = 10 \log \frac{P_1}{P_2}$$
$$= 20 \log \frac{E_1}{E_2}$$
$$= 20 \log \frac{I_1}{I_2}$$

UNEQUAL IMPEDANCES

$$db = 10 \log \frac{P_1}{P_2}$$
$$= 20 \log \frac{E_1 \sqrt{Z_2}}{E_2 \sqrt{Z_1}}$$
$$= 20 \log \frac{I_1 \sqrt{Z_1}}{I_2 \sqrt{Z_2}}$$

EFFICIENCY OF ANY DEVICE

$$\text{Eff} = \frac{\text{Output}}{\text{Input}}$$

Q (QUALITY FACTOR OR FIGURE OF MERIT)

$$Q = \frac{X_l}{R} = \frac{X_C}{R}$$

TRANSFORMER RELATIONSHIPS

$$\frac{Np}{Ns} = \frac{Ep}{Es} = \frac{Is}{Ip} = \sqrt{\frac{Zp}{Zs}}$$

FREQUENCY AND WAVELENGTH

$$f = \frac{1}{t} \qquad t = \frac{1}{f}$$

$$\lambda \text{ (meters)} = \frac{300\,000\,000}{f} \qquad \lambda \text{ (feet)} = \frac{984\,000\,000}{f}$$

Glossary of EDP-Communications Terms

'A'

ABACUS A device for performing calculations by moving beads or counters along rods.

ACCESS TIME The time interval between the request for information and the instant of delivery, i.e., the read or write time of a computer.

ACU See AUTOMATIC CALLING UNIT.

ADDRESS The coded destination of a message.

ADJACENT CHANNEL The information channel which occupies the portion of the frequency spectrum above or below the channel of interest.

ADJACENT CHANNEL INTERFERENCE Noise, crosstalk, or distortion in a reference channel caused by operation of an adjacent channel.

ALTERNATE ROUTE A secondary communications channel for use when the primary channel is inadequate or unavailable.

AMPLIFIER An active circuit designed to increase the power level of a given band of frequencies.

AMPLITUDE The magnitude of variation of a quantity (e.g., voltage) from its zero value.

AMPLITUDE DISTORTION Distortion of the peak positive or negative values of a waveform in respect to the remainder of the waveform. Often called nonlinear distortion.

AMPLITUDE MODULATION The process of combining a low frequency (intelligence) signal with a high frequency (carrier) signal to produce sidebands which represent the intelligence signal. The amplitude of the modulated waveform varies in proportion to the amplitude and frequency of the modulating waveform.

ANGLE MODULATION Frequency of phase modulation.

ANSWERBACK An indication from the receiving business machine that it is ready to accept data from the sending business machine.

A.S.C.I.I. See U.S.A.S.C.I.I.

ASR Abbreviation of "automatic send and receive."

ASYCHRONOUS Not having a constant period. A digital data-transmission format in which start and stop bits identify the beginning and ending of each character. The time interval between characters may vary.

ATTENUATION Power loss in a circuit in which all frequencies under consideration are affected equally. The difference between transmitted and received power.

ATTENUATION DISTORTION A departure from uniform amplification or attenuation over the frequency range required for transmission. A difference in gain at some frequencies within the bandpass of the circuits.

ATTENUATION FREQUENCY DISTORTION The effect which a circuit with limited bandpass will produce upon a complex waveform. Elimination of some of the frequencies in a complex waveform resulting in the output differing from the input waveform.

AUDIO Frequencies within the range of human hearing. Normally considered to include the frequency range between 20 and 20 000 Hz.

AUTOMATIC CALLING UNIT (ACU) A dialing device which permits the business machine to automatically dial calls.

AUTOMATIC STATION SELECTION Used with dial teletype systems. Permits placing and completing of teletype calls without operator intervention.

'B'

BALANCED CIRCUIT Refers to a 2-wire circuit in which the voltages and currents on the wires are electrical opposites in respect to signal ground.

BALANCED MIXER A special circuit using diodes and transformers for the demodulation of a single-sideband waveform. A sideband signal is combined with a reinserted carrier to produce the original audio waveform.

BALANCED MODULATOR A special circuit used in sideband transmitters. It combines a modulating audio waveform with a carrier waveform in such a manner that the output waveform is composed of an upper sideband, lower sideband, and a suppressed carrier.

BAND A range of frequencies under consideration. See BANDPASS, BANDWIDTH.

BANDPASS A description of the frequencies to which a circuit will respond. Normally stated as the upper and lower frequency limits, e.g., 200 Hz to 3200 Hz.

BANDPASS FILTER A circuit which permits passage of a selected range of frequencies and attenuates all frequencies outside this range.

BAND-REJECT FILTER An electrical circuit which permits passage of all frequencies except those within a selected range.

BAND, GUARD See GUARD BAND.

BAND, BROAD See BROAD BAND.

BAND, NARROW See NARROW BAND.

BAND, V-F See VOICE FREQUENCY.

BANDWIDTH A statement of the range of frequencies to which a circuit will respond. Computed by subtracting the lower frequency from the higher frequency of the circuit bandpass.

BASEBAND The frequency range occupied by the aggregate of the transmitted signals used to modulate a carrier.

BATCH PROCESSING A data-processing technique of accumulating similar items for processing together.

BAUD A unit of signaling speed equal to 1 second divided by the time duration of the shortest unit or pulse in any one character.

BAUDOT CODE A 5-bit teletype code named after Emile Baudot, a pioneer in printing telegraphy.

BAUD RATE The number of bits per second of a teletype or data signal based upon the time duration of the shortest bit. In computer systems, the "bit rate" equals the "baud rate" if all bits have the same time duration.

BIT An abbreviation of "binary digit." A single pulse in a group of pulses.

BIT RATE See BAUD RATE.

BLOCK A set of words, characters, or digits, handled as a unit by a computer.

BREAK FEATURE In teletype systems, if the receiving teletypewriter should cease to function, permits the receiving operator to signal the transmitting teletype unit to stop sending.

BRIDGE (1) The shunting of one electrical circuit by another. (2) A circuit arrangement permitting coupling of two or more circuits, ideally providing the least nominal isolation and impedance matching.

BROADBAND A term applied to a facility or circuit which has bandwidth in excess of that required for high-grade voice communications.

BROADCAST Similar to multipoint operation. A transmitting station sends identical information to a number of receiving stations simultaneously.

BUFFER (Data Circuit) A storage device which compensates for a difference in rate of data flow. A circuit or system which stores units or groups of data until it can be used by the receiving machine.

BUFFER (Electrical Function) A circuit which provides electrical isolation between two other circuits, preventing interaction between a driven and a driving circuit.

BUSY HOUR The 60-minute period of the business day when the maximum amount of communications traffic is handled.

BYTE A single group of bits processed together (in parallel). The number of bits in a byte varies with business machine and manufacturer, but is fixed within a given machine.

'C'

CABLE, COAXIAL A small conducting (copper) tube or wire within, and insulated from, another conductor which has a larger diameter.

CABLE, COMBINATION Multiconductor cable in which the wires are grouped into pairs or quads (2- or 4-wire sets).

CABLE, COMPOSITE Cable in which the conductors grouped in one sheath are of different types, gauges, or both.

CABLE, MULTICONDUCTOR An assembly of two or more conductors within a protective sheath, and so arranged that the conductors can be used separately or in groups.

CARRIER (1) In communications, the company or facilities which provide the communications path. (2) A high frequency signal of constant amplitude, frequency, and phase which can be modulated by changing amplitude, frequency, or phase.

CARRIER SHIFT The difference between the steady state mark and space frequencies in a system using frequency shift keyed modulation.

CARRIER TERMINAL EQUIPMENT The multiplexing and demultiplexing equipment, owned and operated by the telephone company or common carrier, which combines the channels for transmission and separates channels after transmission.

C.C.I.T.T. International Telegraph and Telephone Consultative Committee, a committee of the International Telecommunications Union of the United Nations organized to investigate data and teletype communications with the objective of proposing communications standards.

CENTRAL OFFICE The location of switching, dialing, and ringing equipment which provides telephone service to subscribers within an exchange.

CHANNEL A communications link. An electrical or electronic circuit through which intelligence signals are transmitted, and in which the bandwidth and bandpass are defined quantities.

CHANNEL CAPACITY A data term which describes the number of bits per second that a circuit can handle, based upon the circuit bandwidth and noise.

CHANNEL, FOUR-WIRE A communications channel designed for full-duplex operation. Four wires are provided at each termination, two for sending information and two for receiving information.

CHANNEL, TWO-WIRE A communications circuit designed for simplex or half-duplex operation. Two wires are provided at each termination and, with the exception of reverse channel circuits, information is usually transmitted in only one direction at a time.

CHANNEL, VOICE-GRADE A communications channel which has sufficient bandpass and bandwidth to permit voice communications, and which has tolerable amounts of attenuation frequency distortion. A channel frequency compromise between ideal bandpass and acceptable bandpass for the transmission of speech signals.

CHARACTER In computers and business machines, a combination of bits which represent a letter, number, or symbol.

CHARACTERISTIC The integer or "whole-number" part of a logarithm.

CIRCUIT See CHANNEL.

CLOCK (1) Periodic signals used for synchronization. (2) A device that measures time. (3) Equipment or circuits which provide a time base in a system for controlling functions such as counting and sampling.

CODE A system for representing elemental parts of information in a different form. A representative language that can be understood and used by computers and other business machines.

COMMON CARRIER See CARRIER.

COMPANDER An electrical circuit used in the transmission and reception of speech for the purpose of improving the signal-to-noise ratio. Composed of two sections, a COMPRESSOR and an EXPANDER.

COMPRESSOR An electrical circuit which has nonlinear gain, and which is used before transmission to reduce the nominal amplitude range of speech signals. The compressor attenuates high amplitude signals and amplifies weak signals.

CONVERSATION MODE Communications between a computer and terminal unit in which each entry from the terminal elicits a response from the computer and vice versa.

CROSS MODULATION A type of intermodulation that occurs when the desired signal carrier is modulated by an undesirable signal.

CROSSTALK Interference which appears in a given transmitting or recording channel but has its origin in another channel.

CUTOFF FREQUENCY In filters or circuits, the frequency or frequencies at which attenuation begins to rise sharply.

CYCLE An event that recurs at regular intervals. In electrical waveforms, the change of an alternating current waveform from zero through its peak positive, zero, peak negative, and back to zero values. The number of Hertz (cycles per second) is called the frequency of a waveform.

'D'

DAMPING A characteristic built into electrical or mechanical systems which prevents rapid or excessive corrections, and which reduces instability or the tendency to oscillate.

DATA A general term for information consisting of numbers, letters, and symbols.

DATA COLLECTION The act of compiling data from one or more points at a central location.

DATA COMMUNICATIONS The movement of encoded information by electrical transmission.

DATA-PHONE A service mark and trademark of the Bell System. As a service mark, it indicates the use of the Bell System message network for the transmission of data. As a trademark, the brand of data sets manufactured for the DATA-PHONE service.

DATA PROCESSING Any operation or combination of operations on data.

DATA SERVICE The offering by telephone companies to provide data communications over narrowband, voiceband, or broadband circuits.

DATA SET See MODEM.

DATA TERMINAL Data processing equipment that serves as a point for collection, use, or transfer of data signals.

DBM A ratio of a.c. power gain or loss based on a reference of 1 milliwatt of power developed across an impedance of 600 ohms.

DBRN A unit of measure of random-noise amplitude based on a reference level of minus 90 dbm.

DECIBEL (DB) A ratio of a.c. power gain or loss, expressed in bels and decimal parts of bels, based on a comparison of measured output power to reference input power.

DELAY The time required for a signal to pass through a device or circuit.

DELAY DISTORTION The difference in arrival times of two signals of different frequency which have been transmitted simultaneously.

DEMODULATION The process of separating the original modulating waveform from the carrier waveform of a modulated signal or envelope.

DEMODULATOR The circuit or circuits which accomplish demodulation.

DESERIALIZE The conversion from serial-by-bit, serial-by-character data format to parallel-by-bit, serial-by-character data format.

DIAL-UP The use of a dial or pushbutton telephone to initiate a station-to-station call.

DIRECT DISTANCE DIALING A telephone service which permits subscribers to place long distance calls without the aid of an operator.

DISCRIMINATOR A frequency sensitive circuit used for demodulating FM or FSK moduled waveforms.

DISPERSION Separation of a complex waveform into its component frequencies.

DISPERSION, ANOMALOUS A characteristic of a transmission medium in which high frequencies travel with greater velocity than low frequencies.

DISPERSION, NORMAL A characteristic of a transmission medium in which low frequencies travel with greater velocity than high frequencies.

DISPLAY UNIT A device which provides visual representation of data.

DISTORTION Any change in the received-signal waveform compared to the original transmitted-signal waveform.

DROPOUT Separate and distinct variations in signal level which may cause an error in the received or recorded data.

DUPLEX, FULL An arrangement of circuit facilities which permits simultaneous two-way communications.

DUPLEX, HALF An arrangement of circuit facilities which permits transmission in either direction, but in only one direction at a time.

'E'

ECHO A waveform which has been reflected or otherwise returned with sufficient magnitude or delay to be distinguishable from the directly transmitted wave.

ECHO CHECK A method of testing the accuracy of received data by returning it to the sending end of the circuit for comparison with the original data.

ECHO SUPPRESSOR An electronic circuit used in 4-wire trunk lines to disable the return path when information is being transmitted.

END OF MESSAGE (EOM) A data character which indicates to the receiving device that the final data has been transmitted.

ENVELOPE Refers to the overall shape of a modulated waveform, or to the frequency content of a modulated waveform if the amplitude is constant.

ENVELOPE DELAY A measure of the delay distortion which occurs when a narrowband amplitude-modulated waveform is transmitted through the circuit under test.

ENVELOPE DELAY DISTORTION The characteristic envelope delay curve of a circuit. It is produced by testing for envelope delay at various points within the channel bandpass. The maximum deviation of the envelope delay curve within the circuit bandpass is often quoted as a circuit parameter.

EOM End Of Message.

EQUALIZATION, AMPLITUDE The introduction of gain or loss characteristics into a circuit to compensate for the frequency response characteristic of the circuit.

EQUALIZATION, DELAY The introduction of additional phase shift into a circuit at frequencies which, without equalization, undergo lesser amounts of delay.

EQUALIZER A circuit used for equalizing line characteristics. A compensating network.

ERROR A mistake in transmission. A false transformation of information.

ERROR CONTROL A circuit arrangement that will detect errors in the received data, and may correct the errors by performing operations on the received data or by retransmission from the source.

ERROR RATE The number of errors which occur in a system in a fixed amount of time.

EXCHANGE A part of a telephone system composed of one central office, the subscribers which it serves, and the interconnecting lines or wires.

EXPANDER The part of a compander which, because of its nonlinear gain, reproduces speech signals occupying the normal amplitude range from signals which have been compressed for transmission.

EXCLUSION KEY In a dial-up operation, the mechanical key or switch which transfers the MODEM in and out of the telephone circuit, permitting voice or data operation.

'F'

FACILITY A circuit or channel, or an identifiable section of a circuit or channel.

FACSIMILE A likeness of representation of pictures or printed material, or any 2-dimensional image in graphic form.

FASCIMILE TRANSMISSION The process of scanning an image at the transmitter, converting the image to elemental electrical signals for transmission, and reconstructing the image on film or treated paper at the receiving station.

FILTER See BANDPASS, BAND REJECT, HIGH PASS, LOW PASS.

FLIP FLOP A bistable multivibrator. A circuit which will remain in either of two stable states until application of an external signal causes it to change.

FOREIGN EXCHANGE SERVICE A service which connects a subscriber telephone to a remote exchange, providing the equivalent of local service from the distant exchange.

FORM FEED A device which correctly positions documents or business forms in teletype units, printers, or other business machines.

FOUR WIRE See CHANNEL.

FREQUENCY The repetition rate of a periodically recurring waveform, commonly expressed in Hertz (Hz) or cycles-per-second (cps).

FREQUENCY DISTORTION See ATTENUATION DISTORTION, ATTENUATION FREQUENCY DISTORTION.

FREQUENCY DIVISION MULTIPLEXING A technique of using carrier generators, mixers, bandpass filters, and hybrid circuits to combine many channels of information for transmission. Separation of channels is accomplished by demultiplexing.

FREQUENCY MODULATION The process of varying the frequency of a carrier waveform with the amount and rate of deviation being proportional to the amplitude and frequency of the modulating audio waveform.

FREQUENCY SHIFT KEYING (FSK) A form of frequency modulation in which the modulating waveform causes the output frequency to shift between two predetermined values, and in which the output waveform has no phase discontinuity.

FREQUENCY TRANSLATION The transfer of signals occupying a definite frequency band, channel, or group of channels, from one position in the frequency spectrum to another, in such a manner that the arithmetic frequency difference of the signals within the band or channels is unaltered.

'G'

GATE A circuit which has one output and one or more inputs, the output being energized only under certain input conditions.

GUARD BAND An unused section of the frequency spectrum between channels. A method of preventing adjacent channel interference.

'H'

HARD COPY A printed copy produced by a machine in readable form, i.e., reports, listings, summaries.

HARMONIC A sinusoidal waveform which is an integral multiple of a fundamental-frequency waveform. A waveform twice the frequency of the fundamental is called the second harmonic.

HETERODYNE The process of combining two frequencies in a nonlinear mixer to produce a distorted waveform at the output which contains the sum frequency, the difference frequency, and both of the original frequencies.

HIGH-PASS FILTER An electrical circuit which permits passage of higher frequencies, sharply attenuating those below a certain cutoff frequency.

HOLDING TIME The total time a communications channel is in use for a communication, including both message and operating time.

HYBRID CIRCUIT A linear mixer which combines waveforms without heterodyning.

HYBRID COIL A transformer which has essentially three pairs of balanced coils mounted on a common core in such a manner as to prevent feedback or oscillations.

'I'

IMPEDANCE The quantity of opposition to a.c. current flow, expressed in ohms, offered by a circuit or transmission line which has both resistance and reactance parameters.

IMPEDANCE MATCH Describes a situation in which the source, line, and load impedances of a circuit are made nearly the same, and which results in the most efficient operation of the circuit.

IMPEDANCE MISMATCH A circuit fault which results when dissimilar impedances are connected together, and which may result in excessive power loss, poor frequency response, and generally degraded circuit operation.

IMPULSE NOISE The number of impulses per unit of time in a circuit which exceed a predetermined threshold level.

IMPULSES High-density, short-duration electric currents or magnetic fields.

INFORMATION Data, or a message. A combination of fundamental elements into a form which can be interpreted.

INFORMATION RETRIEVAL The method or procedures for recovering specific information from stored data.

INPUT Signals supplied to equipment in an appropriate form for storage, processing, control, or transmission. The section or terminals of equipment where signals first appear.

INSERTION LOSS A power loss which normally occurs because of the physical interconnection of circuits.

INTERFACE The physical point of interconnection; i.e., terminal boards and plugs between units of equipment or systems.

INTERRUPT An intentional break in the normal data flow within a system, so that the flow of data can be resumed at that point at some later time. Interrupts normally permit a computer to service a peripheral device.

'J'

JITTER An instability of the transitions from mark to space frequency or from space to mark frequency of a FSK data signal. The instability is reflected in the demodulated data waveform as variations in the position of the leading and trailing edges.

'K'

KILO A prefix indicating that the fundamental unit is multipled by 1 000.

'L'

LEASED CHANNEL A point-to-point or multipoint circuit reserved for the sole use of the leasing subscriber.

LEVEL The quantity of power in watts at some particular point in a circuit, or an indication of the absolute signal level expressed in watts, volts, or amperes compared to an arbitrary reference level.

LEVEL CONVERTER A circuit which changes the voltage levels of d.c. data signals, and which may also invert the polarity of the signals.

LINE See CHANNEL.

LINE COORDINATION The process of ensuring that equipment at each end of a communications circuit is prepared for a specific transmission.

LINE FEED A function code which causes rotation of the platen of a printing machine to position the paper for the next line of print.

LINE HIT Rapid spurious signals or changes in a circuit. An unpredictable, short-duration change in amplitude or phase of signals on a transmission line.

LINE PRINTER A printer in which all characters across an entire line of type are printed in one machine cycle.

LINE SPEED The maximum rate at which data signals may be transmitted through a given channel, stated in bits-per-second or baud rate.

LINK See CHANNEL.

LISSAJOUS PATTERN Refers to the display on a cathode-ray tube when signal voltages of various amplitude and phase relationships are applied simultaneously to the vertical and horizontal deflection circuits.

LOAD (1) The power consumed by a system or circuit which is performing its function. (2) The input impedance of a device which is connected to the output of a transmission line. (3) The act of connecting a terminating impedance to a line or circuit.

LOADING In telephone circuits, the intentional introduction of lumped values of reactance (usually inductance) into the transmission line to alter and improve the electrical characteristics for the purpose at hand.

LOOP A closed path. In communications circuits, any closed section, segment, or facility of the transmission medium.

LOOPBACK The technique of returning received signals to their source over a separate channel, line, or route.

LOOP GAIN (LOSS) The sum of the power gains and losses incurred by a signal in passing through a closed circuit or loop.

LOW-PASS FILTER An electrical circuit which permits passage of lower frequencies, sharply attenuating those above a certain cutoff frequency.

LOW SPEED A transmission rate, normally limited to a maximum of 200 bits-per-second.

'M'

MAKE-BREAK OPERATION Producing a series of current pulses by opening and closing electrical contacts in a circuit.

MANTISSA The decimal part of a logarithm, obtained from an appropriate table.

MARK One of two possible conditions. A closed line in a neutral circuit. The lower frequency of an FSK waveform.

MARKING Originally indicated a closed key in telegraphy. Presently implies (1) presence of current in a communication circuit, (2) the idle condition of a teletypewriter, (3) the binary digit ONE in computer language, (4) the application of the mark frequency to a communications circuit.

MEMORY A general term for equipment which holds or stores machine-readable data.

MESSAGE See INFORMATION.

MESSAGE FORMAT Rules for placement of separate portions of a message, such as heading address, text, and EOM.

MESSAGE SWITCHING Data transmission in separate circuits by routing the data through a central point.

MICROWAVE A form of radio communications in which the wavelength of the radio-frequency carrier signals is less than one meter.

MIXER, LINEAR A circuit which combines two frequencies, producing the instantaneous sum of their voltages at the output, and which does not cause heterodyning.

MIXER, NON-LINEAR A circuit which combines two frequencies, producing at the output the sum, difference, and original frequencies.

MNEMONIC Information coded in such a manner as to assist the human memory.

MODE Method of operation.

MODEM Acronym for modulator/demodulator. A data set. An equipment designed to produce FSK waveforms from d.c. data waveforms in the modulator section, and to produce d.c. waveforms from FSK waveforms in the demodulator section.

MODULATION The process or causing variations in the amplitude, frequency, or phase of a carrier waveform in proportion to the characteristics of a modulating waveform.

MODULATION ENVELOPE See ENVELOPE.

MODULATOR The circuit or group of circuits responsible for causing modulation.

MULTICHANNEL Describes the capability for simultaneous transmission through the same transmission medium of more than one intelligence waveform with facilities for separating the channels after transmission.

MULTIPLEXING The process of combining two or more channels of information for simultaneous transmission.

MULTIPOINT A mode of communications circuit operation in which signals within the circuit are received by all (more than two) stations connected to the circuit.

'N'

NARROWBAND Describes a communications circuit which, because of its limited bandpass and bandwidth, permits data communications at a maximum rate of approximately 200 baud.

NET LOSS The sum of the power gains and losses between two terminations of a telephone circuit.

NEUTRAL KEYING A form of telegraphy in which the circuit current is either ON or OFF. When current flows the condition is called a MARK. When no current flows the condition is referred to as a SPACE.

NOISE Undesirable and unintelligible electrical disturbances present at the receive termination of a communications circuit.

NOISE LEVEL The power level of noise waveforms, expressed in watts, dbm, dbrn, or volts, measured at a particular point in a communications circuit.

'O'

OFFLINE Pertaining to equipment or devices which function without direct control by the central processing unit.

ONLINE Pertaining to equipment functions performed in peripheral equipment which is under direct control of the central processing unit.

OPM A teletype term meaning operations-per-minute. Similar to characters-per-minute in data terminology.

OUTPUT (1) The information which is generated by a computer or data processing unit. (2) The signals which leave a unit of equipment destined for use at a different location or in different equipment.

'P'

PAD A network of selected resistors connected in a configuration which matches unequal circuit impedances or inserts a fixed attenuation loss in the circuit.

PARALLEL TRANSMISSION A method of information transfer in which each bit or character is sent simultaneously through separate circuits, or through separate sections of the same circuit.

PARITY BIT A binary digit added to a character to make the sum of the bits odd or even.

PARITY CHECK Testing of the ONES or ZEROES in a

character to determine whether the parity remains correct during transmission.

PARTY LINE A single telephone circuit serving two or more subscribers.

PASSBAND See BANDPASS.

PATH See CHANNEL.

PERFORATOR A keyboard device for punching paper tape.

PERIPHERAL UNITS Equipment which works in conjunction with a data terminal or computer, but is not part of that unit.

PHASE MODULATION The process of changing the phase of a carrier waveform in proportion to the amplitude and frequency of the modulating waveform.

PHASE SHIFT The difference between corresponding points on input and output waveforms, expressed in degrees, and independent of amplitude.

POLAR KEYING - POLAR OPERATION A form of telegraphy in which circuit current flows in one direction for marking, and the opposite direction for spacing. A circuit in which the mark and space transitions are represented by a current reversal.

POLL, POLLING A method of permitting stations in a multipoint circuit to transmit without contending for the line. Sequential testing from a central location to decide which terminal device uses the circuit.

PRINT OUT See HARD COPY.

PRIVATE LINE See LEASED CHANNEL.

PROCESSING, REAL TIME A speed sufficient to provide an answer within the actual time the problem must be solved. The actual time during which a process or computation takes place.

PULSE AMPLITUDE MODULATION The process of amplitude modulating a pulse carrier waveform. Abbreviated PAM.

PULSE CODE MODULATION A modulation process in which the signal is sampled periodically. Each sample is quantized and transmitted as a binary code. Abbreviated PCM.

'Q'

Q or QUALITY FACTOR A measure of the frequency selectivity of a mechanical or electrical system. An indication of the sharpness of resonance of a circuit.

QUARTER SPEED Refers to the transmission of data in systems at one-fourth the speed of associated equipment.

'R'

RADIO Communications by electromagnetic waves propagated through space.

RADIO FREQUENCY A general term applied to the use of electromagnetic waves between 10 kHz and 3 000 gHz.

RANGE, FREQUENCY See RESPONSE.

READ The process of acquiring information from a storage device.

READOUT Output information from a computer or business machine in the form of visual displays, printed pages, punched cards or tape, etc.

REAL TIME The actual time during which a physical process takes place.

RECEIVE ONLY (RO) Service in which the terminal equipment is capable of receiving signals but does not have a transmit capability.

RECEIVER A device which accepts information from the transmission medium and converts it to meaningful form.

RECORD One or more characters that are grouped together in the system data flow.

REFLECTION See ECHO.

REMOTE START Indicates an ability to activate equipment from a distant location.

REMOTE TERMINAL Any terminal in a communications network other than the terminal at which a person is physically located.

REPEATER A telephone-line amplifier and associated hybrid and balance circuits.

RESONANCE A circuit condition which, at the applied frequency, produces equal and opposite amounts of capacitive reactance and inductive reactance. A resonant circuit is described as "tuned," and may provide maximum gain or maximum loss depending on the circuit configuration.

RESPONSE, FREQUENCY An expression of the output of a device or circuit as a function of the input, under conditions which must be explicitly stated. A plot of output versus frequency for a particular device or circuit.

RESPONSE TIME Elapsed time between generation of an inquiry at a data terminal and receipt of a response at the same terminal.

RETURN LOSS The difference between the power incident upon, and the power reflected from, an impedance discontinuity. The power remaining after a portion has been reflected from a point of impedance mismatch.

REVERSE CHANNEL An error-control feature incorporated into some MODEMS which permits transmission of error-control data over a 2-wire line at the same time as, and in the opposite direction from, normal data flow.

R O See RECEIVE ONLY.

'S'

SAMPLING Periodically recording the instantaneous value of a continuously varying quantity.

SCANNER An equipment which periodically checks each site on a leased line for message traffic or message availability.

SELECTIVE CALLING A communications arrangement in which a transmitting station is able to specify which of several stations on the same line is to receive a message.

SEND To transmit or make information available for transmission. A transmitting machine can be sending, even though the information is not being received.

SERIAL Pertaining to the time sequencing of two or more processes in the same facility. Sequential processing or transmission of fundamental elements of information.

SERIAL TRANSMISSION A method of information transfer in which each bit of a character follows preceding bits in time, and each character of a message follows preceding characters in time. The first bit of the first character precedes the second bit of the first character, which precedes the second character, etc.

SIDEBAND A frequency generated by a mixer which has two other frequencies as input signals. The upper sideband is equal to the arithmetic sum of the input frequencies, and the lower sideband is equal to the arithmetic difference between the two input frequencies.

SIGNAL A visual, audible, or other means of conveying information. The information, message, or effect transferred by a communication system. A signal wave. The physical embodiment of a message.

SIGNAL-TO-NOISE RATIO (SNR) A ratio of the magnitude of the signal to that of the noise at a given point of measurement.

SIMPLEX A communications facility capable of transferring information in one direction only, or a mode of circuit operation which permits communications in one direction only, even though the circuit may be designed for half-duplex operation.

SKIN EFFECT Describes the tendency of high-frequency a.c. signals to cause current to flow nearer the surface of a conductor, effectively increasing the resistance of the conductor.

SOLID STATE A circuit composed of transistors, diodes, and passive components.

SPACE One of two possible conditions. An open line in a neutral circuit. The higher of two frequencies of an FSK waveform.

SPACING Continuous application to the communications circuit of the space condition or frequency. Transmission of a sequence of ZERO bits.

SPECTRUM, FREQUENCY A continuous range of electromagnetic radiations.

SPEED See TRANSMISSION RATE, VELOCITY OF PROPAGATION, THROUGHPUT.

SR Abbreviation of Send-Receive.

START BIT A supplemental data-bit added at the beginning of each character of asynchronously transmitted data to indicate the beginning of the character.

STATION One of the input or output points of a communication system.

STOP BIT A supplemental bit added at the end of each character of asynchronously transmitted data to indicate that transmission of the character is complete.

STORAGE A general term for any device capable of retaining information.

STORE AND FORWARD A process of message handling used in a message switching system.

STUNT BOX A device to control nonprinting functions of a teletypewriter terminal.

SUBSCRIBER A person who receives, and pays for, services provided by a system.

SUBSCRIBER STATION The location of equipment which the subscriber uses to access the communications network.

SWITCHING The process of establishing temporary interconnections between two or more stations of a communications system.

SWITCHING CIRCUIT An arrangement of relays, switches, etc., which establishes continuity through a communications circuit before communications begin.

SYNCHRONOUS In step or in phase, as applied to two devices or signals. In a synchronous data transmission system, a separate clocking waveform is used to identify individual characters and blocks of characters, and to initiate function, storage, and control signals in respect to the transmitted data.

'T'

TARIFF The published rate for a specific unit of equipment, facility, or service which a telephone company provides.

TD See TRANSMITTER DISTRIBUTOR.

TELEGRAPH, TELEGRAPHY A system of transmitting, receiving, and printing graphic symbols or images without graduation of shade values.

TELEPAK A leased wideband channel offering by A.T. & T.

TELEPHONE An apparatus which includes a microphone and a speaker. The microphone converts sound energy to electrical signals which are transmitted. At the receiving telephone, the speaker converts these electrical signals to related sounds.

TELEPRINTER A trade name used by Western Union for its telegraph terminal equipment. A teletype-signal receiving and printing device.

TELETYPE A system of communicating printed information using keyboard or paper-tape transmitting devices and receiving printing devices.

TELETYPE CORPORATION A subsidiary of Western Electric Corporation which manufactures teletype and switching equipment.

TELETYPE GRADE CHANNEL The lowest-quality narrowband channel in terms of speed, cost, and accuracy.

TELETYPEWRITER A term which applies to equipment made by the Teletype Corporation and to teleprinter equipment.

TELEX An automatic teletype exchange service provided by Western Union.

TERMINAL A point at which signals can enter into or exit from a system or communications network.

TERMINAL UNIT Equipment which has access to a communications channel for the purpose of providing input or accepting output signals from the channel.

TEXT The body of a message. The substantive information which is conveyed.

THROUGHPUT EDP term indicating the ability of a system, circuit, or unit of equipment to handle rate or volume of data.

TIME DIVISION MULTIPLEX A process for the simultaneous transmission of two or more information signals in which elemental parts of each information signal is sampled. The samples are sequentially applied for transmission, and the information signals are reconstructed from the samples after transmission.

TRANSCEIVER A single unit of equipment which has both a transmitting and a receiving capability.

TRANSCRIBER Equipment associated with data processing which converts records of information from one machine language to another, or to a different form, without altering the content of the record.

TRANSDUCER Any device which converts energy from one form to another, i.e., a microphone or speaker.

TRANSFER, PARALLEL See PARALLEL TRANSMISSION.

TRANSFER, SERIAL See SERIAL TRANSMISSION.

TRANSITION A change from one steady-state condition of a voltage or frequency to a different steady-state condition of voltage or frequency. The period of time required to effect the change.

TRANSLATOR A device which transforms signals from the form in which they were generated to some other form, i.e., one machine language to another.

TRANSMISSION Modulation of a transmission medium by an intelligence signal and physical transfer of the information across a distance.

TRANSMISSION, ASYNCHRONOUS See ASYNCHRONOUS.

TRANSMISSION RATE The number of information elements sent per unit of time, usually expressed as bits, baud, characters, words, blocks, or records per second or minute.

TRANSMISSION, SYNCHRONOUS See SYNCHRONOUS.

TRANSMITTER A unit of equipment that converts

202

information to a form which will be accepted by the transmission medium.

TRANSMITTER DISTRIBUTOR A motor driven device which translates teletype-coded information from punched paper tape into electrical impulses which are transmitted to one or more receiving stations.

TRUNK A communications channel between two different offices, or between groups of equipment within the same office.

TURN-AROUND TIME The time required to reverse the direction of transmission in a half-duplex communications circuit.

TWO-WIRE CIRCUIT See CHANNEL.

TWX A 60 or 100 word-per-minute Bell System telecommunications network.

'U'

U.S.A.S.C.I.I. American Standard Code for Information Interchange. A code recommended by the American Standards Association for the digital transmission of information.

'V'

VELOCITY FACTOR A ratio of the actual velocity of a wave along a conductor to the velocity of a wave through free space.

VELOCITY OF PROPAGATION The speed, expressed in distance per unit of time, at which electrical or electromagnetic signals pass through a transmission medium.

VOICE FREQUENCY (V-F) The frequency range from about 20 to 8 000 Hz inclusive. The repetition rates of mechanical vibrations generated by human vocal cords as speech.

VOICE-FREQUENCY CHANNEL A communications channel which has sufficient bandwidth for the transmission of intelligible speech signals, normally 200 to 3 200 Hz.

VOICE-GRADE CHANNEL Describes a communications channel which is adequate for voice communications, regardless of the purpose for which the channel is used

'W'

WADS Abbreviation for Wide Area Data Service. A plan by A.T. & T. to lease teletype grade channels on a dial-up basis from many points in the country.

WATS Abbreviation for Wide Area Telephone Service. A telephone service which permits subscribers to dial directly any of six bands or zones within the United States for a flat monthly charge.

WAVE, CARRIER See CARRIER.

WAY STATION A telegraph term for one of the stations in a multipoint circuit.

WEIGHTING Shaping or limiting the frequency response of a circuit for the purpose at hand.

WIDEBAND See BROADBAND.

WORD In teletype-signal formats, a word that is composed of six characters, five letters, numbers, or symbols and a space. Word length in computer systems and business machines varies.

WPM Words per minute. Describes transmission rates of teletype systems. Speeds of 60- and 100-wpm are common.

WRITE The process of recording information on a storage device such as magnetic tape, drum, or disc, or in the memory section of a computer.

ANSWERS TO QUESTIONS

SECTION A

1. Vision and hearing

2. Limitations of the basic senses i.e.; distance, speed, volume

3. Formulation, generation, transmission, reception, and interpretation of a message.

4. Parts or elements

5. Physical transfer and interpretation of information

SECTION B

1. Control section, ALU, and memory

2. Input devices, output devices, file storage devices, central processing unit

3. A system which responds immediately to commands and performs operations under direct control of the CPU.

4. Remotely located equipment can be in almost instantaneous contact with a centrally located computer center and file storage equipment.

SECTION C

1. A person who receives and pays for services provided by a system

2. Reduces the number of wires or lines required in a telephone system and provides more economical use of existing lines

3. Central office equipment, subscriber equipment, and interconnecting lines

4. Dialing, ringing, and selection of other telephones within the exchange and access to interoffice and toll trunks

5. Open wire lines, multiconductor cables, undersea cables, microwave (Radio) systems

6. A single path or route through which one or more intelligence signals may be transferred at a given time

SECTION D

1. A simple electrical circuit is a closed path through which current flows, while a communications circuit may include many different transmission mediums.

2a. Transmission is possible in one direction only

b. Transmission is possible in one direction or the other

c. Simultaneous transmission in both directions is possible.

3. In unbalanced circuits one of the wires is electrical ground or zero, but in balanced lines, neither wire is eiectrically zero and voltages on the wires are equal and out of phase.

4. Public switched lines are not permanently connected and require d.c. voltages to operate. Dedicated lines are permanently connected and d.c. voltages are not applied.

5. Multipoint.

SECTION E

1a. 200 to 3200 Hz
b. 3000 Hz

2. Voice, facsimile, teletype and data signals

3. Transmitter distributor and a teletypewriter

4. 74 baud

5. 3000 Hz

6. Character format and transmission rate

7. USASCII

8. Changes d.c. data levels sufficiently to operate the MODEM and provides inversion if necessary.

9. Low speed devices such as the teletype.

10. Broadband service provides for higher transmission rates, but is more expensive than voice-band service.

SECTION F

1. A waveform of constant amplitude, frequency, and phase

2. It is usually discarded or eliminated.

3. AM, FM, SSB, FSK

4. Amplitude variations of the envelope (caused by presence of sidebands)

5. Sum, difference, carrier, and modulating frequencies

6. Frequency deviations of the carrier above or below the rest frequency

7. Greater bandwidth is permitted for the modulating signals.

8. Broader bandwidth is required for FM transmissions.

9. Eliminate the carrier and undesired sideband frequencies using a bandpass filter.

10. Spectrum economy, power conservation, less noise interference

11. D.C. data waveform

12. space

13. marking

14. CF = 1700 Hz
BW = 1000 Hz

15. Eliminates or reduces phase discontinuity

16. Converts FSK signals to d.c. data levels

17. Higher transmission rates are possible in a given channel bandwidth.

SECTION G

1. The process of combining different channels of information for transmission through a part of the transmission medium.

2. FDM and TDM

3. Central offices and toll switchboards

4. Multiplexing and demultiplexing of channels

5. Oscillator, mixer, and bandpass filter

6. To avoid nonlinear mixing (heterodyning)

7. Use of the same frequencies is required for translating channels to their original location in the spectrum.

8. Select desired mixer products while rejecting all other frequencies.

9. Central office switching equipment

10. The frequency response (bandpass and bandwidth) varies with type of medium.

11. yes (coaxial cable or microwave systems)

SECTION H

1. Resistance, reactance, and impedance

2. Resistance

3. Length, diameter, type of material, temperature, (frequency - apparent resistance)

4. Tendency of current to flow near the surface of a conductor at higher frequencies

5. Copper

6. (40 ohm per 1000') x 8 = 320 ohm

7a. Increases
 b. Decreases

8. High

9a. Resistance
 b. XL
 c. XC

10. Impedance varies with frequency, and is only 600 ohm at 1000 Hz.

11. Impedance matching is necessary to ensure maximum transfer of power.

SECTION I

1. One bel indicates one at the power levels is ten times as great as the other.

2. 0.001

3. 20

4. Decibels represent logarithmic quantities of absolute power.

5. 6.0000

6. 1 MW, 600 ohm @ 1000 Hz

7. Circuit impedance, applied frequency, impedance of the meter, waveform of the signal

8a. Peak-to-peak
 b. RMS (effective)

9a. 0.14
 b. -14

10. 9 dbm power loss

11. -14

SECTION J

1. Attenuation

2. Attenuation distortion

3. Compare receive levels at mark and space frequencies. Difference in receive levels indicates frequency response of the circuit.

4. AFD occurs when circuit does not have sufficient bandwidth and bandpass to permit transfer of a complex waveform.

5. Unwanted and unintelligible signals

6. Random noise
 Impulse noise

7. Thermal agitation, atmospheric disturbances, motor and generator fields, circuit elements

8. Appropriate bandpass filter

9. -90 dbm with C message filter

10. -22

11. Counts per unit of time above a reference threshold level

12. Dialing pulses, relay contacts, motor fields

13. In other communications channels which parallel the given channel through some portion of the transmission medium.

14a. Inductive
 b. Capacitive coupling

15. Select alternate channel, select alternate route, or reduce signal level in the interfering channel.

16. Impedance mismatches

17. Distance from source to point of reflection

18. Length

19. Difference in arrival times of two simultaneously transmitted signals

20. Dispersive quality, i.e.; normal or anomalous dispersion

21. EDD is more easily measured and corrected.

22. Approximately 2000 Hz (1700 - 2200 Hz)

23. Lissajous and eye patterns

24. Jitter

25. 5

26. Hits
 Dropouts

27. Insertion loss

SECTION K

1. Overcome attenuation losses
 Maintain signal-to-noise ratio

2. Terminal

3a. Hybrid
 b. Balance

4. They have power loss and are frequency sensitive

5. Balanced to unbalanced conversion
 Bridging
 Isolation

6. Prevents an impedance mismatch between transformer and telephone line

7. Square, H pad, T pad, π pad

8. Low

9. Complex bandpass filter

10. Connection of an appropriate filter to tailor frequency response

11. Compensate for poor frequency response

12. Controls phase shift thereby compensating for delay distortion

13. Terminal repeaters & terminations

14. Half Duplex

15. Improve signal-to-noise ratio of voice circuits

16. Companders may cause excessive attenuation of rapidly changing data signals.

SECTION L

1. Circuit designation, general characteristics, attenuation characteristics, delay characterics, noise characteristics

2. Data only, alternate voice/data, teletype, telephoto, and facsimile operation

3. Type of service, mode of operation, method and impedance of the terminations, maximum signal power level

4. -15 to -17

5. Circuit attenuation varies between normal maintenance periods.

6. Attenuation at 1000 Hz (L) when maximum signal power level is applied to the input

7. Channel B

Freq. Range	Var. (db)
300-499 (L)	-2 to +6
500-2400 (L)	-1 to +3
2401-2700 (L)	-2 to +6

8. Smallest segment of the bandwidth which includes the mark and space frequencies.

9. Channel A

Freq. Range   Env. Delay

800-2800 Hz less than 500 us

10. -45

11. Channel A

90 counts in 1/2 hour
@ 68 dbrn0 6A-VB

SECTION M

1. Interface between EDP and Telephone company equipment

2. Transmitter, receiver, power supply

3. Receiver (demodulator)

4. No, RQS is necessary to modulator operation

5. Presence of a signal in the demodulator section of a MODEM

6. Higher data transfer rates because start and stop bits are not transmitted

7. Parity bits permit receiving equipment to check the validity of received characters.

8. At the end of a block of transmitted characters

9. Reverse and forward data signals occupy different segments of the channel bandwidth.

10. Operational echo suppressors prevent reverse channel information from reaching the sending terminal.

11. Removable jumpers used to make connections inside a MODEM

12. Local business machines and data set

13. Local business machines, data sets at each end of a circuit, and telephone line

14. Replacing the defective circuit board rather than the discrete component

15. No

FINAL EXAM

Questions And Answers		Section Tested	Questions And Answers		Section Tested
1.	b	G	14.	c	L
2.	a	K, F	15.	e	D
3.	d	I	16.	a	M
4.	c	J, L	17.	e	F, M
5.	c	M	18.	d	K, J
6.	b	E	19.	b	H
7.	c	J, L	20.	a	E – F
8.	d	F	21.	e	L, J, K
9.	a	D	22.	d	M, K, J
10.	b	M	23.	b	D
11.	e	J, K, L	24.	a	F
12.	d	I	25.	c	H, K, J
13.	c	M			

TO THE READER

This book is one of the expanding series of Blacksburg Continuing Education books that will cover the field of digital electronics from basic gates and flip-flops through micro-computers and digital telecommunications. We are attempting to develop a mailing list of individuals who would like to receive information on the series. We would be de-lighted to add your name to it if you would fill in the information below. Mail this sheet to Blacksburg Continuing Education Series, P.O. Box 715, Blacksburg, Virginia 24060. Thanks.

1. I have the following books:

☐ 21447 The 8080A Bugbook®: Microcomputer Interfacing and Programming
☐ 21536 DBUG: An 8080 Interpretive Debugger
☐ 21537 Design of Op-Amp Circuits, With Experiments
☐ 21538 555 Timer Applications Sourcebook, With Experiments
☐ 21539 Design of Active Filters, With Experiments
☐ 21540 Microcomputer—Analog Converter Software and Hardware Interfacing
☐ 21541 8080/8085 Software Design
☐ 21542 Logic & Memory Experiments Using TTL Integrated Circuits, Book 1
☐ 21543 Logic & Memory Experiments Using TTL Integrated Circuits, Book 2
☐ 21545 Design of Phase-Locked Loop Circuits, With Experiments
☐ 21546 Interfacing and Scientific Data Communication Experiments
☐ 21547 NCR Data Processing Concepts Course
☐ 21548 NCR Data Communications Concepts
☐ 21549 NCR Basic Electronics Course, With Experiments
☐ 21550 Introductory Experiments in Digital Electronics and 8080A Microcompute Programming and Interfacing, Book 1
☐ 21551 Introductory Experiments in Digital Electronics and 8080A Microcompute Programming and Interfacing, Book 2

2. My occupation is: ☐ student   ☐ teacher, instructor   ☐ hobbyis

   ☐ housewife   ☐ scientist, engineer, doctor, etc.   ☐ businessma

   ☐ Other: _____

Name (print): _____

Address _____

City _____ State _____

Zip Code _____